AMBITIOUS II

AMBITIOUS II

FEAR NO DOUBT, REWIRE, FLY HIGHER

LIKEWISE & VELVET SKIES

Library of Congress Control Number: 2023915497

ISBN: 978-1-954676589
eBook ISBN: 978-1-954676596

Although this publication is designed to provide accurate information about the subject matter, the publisher and the author assume no responsibility for any errors, inaccuracies, omissions, or inconsistencies herein. This publication is intended as a resource; however, it is not intended as a replacement for direct and personalized professional services.

Cover and Interior Design: Emma Elzinga

Printed in the United States of America

First Edition

3 West Garden Street, Ste. 718
Pensacola, FL 32502
www.indigoriverpublishing.com

Ordering Information:

Quantity sales: Special discounts are available on quantity purchases by corporations, associations, and others.
For details, contact the publisher at the address above.

Orders by US trade bookstores and wholesalers:
Please contact the publisher at the address above.

With Indigo River Publishing, you can always expect great books, strong voices, and meaningful messages. Most importantly, you'll always find . . . *words worth reading.*

CONTENTS

CHAPTER ONE

My name is Fear. What a pleasure to meet you! I keep you on your toes, producing great fruit, and if you allow me, I will do even more. It is true that you never know when I will appear. I offer you a lifetime of surprises and can send you panicking around every corner. Just ask Likewise. Running rampant and touching as many lives as possible is the name of my game. I will be absolutely thrilled to manage you if you do not wish to do so yourself. You will see that I am a master at building until you have chronic anxiety and your heart erratically pounds, echoing of a child beating drums.

HAVE YOU EVER BEEN in an uncomfortable situation where your heartbeat sped up as if you were in a wrestling match with yourself? I have. Was there a time when your fears caused your stomach to flip-flop like a live fish on dry land? Have you stood among others to speak, gasping for air as though a plastic bag were on your head? It could be that you unexpectedly became so parched in the process of talking that your tongue suddenly seemed to be glued to the roof of your mouth.

The instant you stepped on stage or before an audience, did self-doubt creep into your mind? Were you experiencing episodes of summertime heatwaves kindled from within? Was sweat oozing from your forehead and trickling onto your face in the manner of an old-fashioned coffee percolator? Perhaps you were certain that an extreme, chill-inducing cold front had taken residence inside your body.

Do you recall being so nervous about something that your hands trembled, similar to an idling vehicle in need of new spark plugs? Could you sense the growing tension creeping from your shoulders into your neck and head as if you were a drawstring sack gradually and tightly being cinched at the top? Did the room begin to twirl like a majorette's baton? Were you able to get a grip on your unsteadiness, or did symptoms progress until you felt ill and were making a mad dash for a restroom?

Fear can be good or bad. It depends not only on what you are doing when it strikes but also on your mindset. In moderation, fear can enhance focus, clarity, and concentration, leading one to prioritize and transform his or her conduct. Sometimes the temporary, sinking feelings of panic and uneasiness give rise to the development of original ideas and solid solutions. Void of extremes, fear has the opportunity to work as intended.

Ideally, fear alerts us to actual and pending dangers so that we can swiftly take appropriate actions to remain safe. Say that you're hiking a rugged trail when you catch a glimpse of a large rattlesnake slithering across your path. You immediately divert your steps in order to save your life. Whether you find yourself driving too fast for road conditions, smelling a gasoline leak, hearing a lifeguard announce, "Beach closure due to riptides," feeling heat from an encroaching fire, or listening to government officials publicize a new epidemic or pandemic, fear mobilizes us to shield ourselves and our loved ones from harm.

Fear is necessary and healthy in limited doses. When it becomes excessive, it can wreak havoc on both the mind and body. Sustained feelings of distress and alarm can stop you in your tracks and steal your ambitiousness. Unbridled fear often leads to chronic anxiety that, in turn, circles back to fear. You do not want to be caught up in this vicious cycle. If you already are, you can learn to overcome. Begin by telling yourself, *I can, and I will!*

CHAPTER TWO

I, Likewise, dealt with my own fear and anxiety beginning at an early age. If you have read *Ambitious: One Man's Journey to Conquer the Darkness of Dyslexia*, you are aware of some of the underlying circumstances that contributed to my angst. Challenging situations seemed to be up and down and all around until they popped out and grabbed me like Stephen King's Pennywise, the Dancing Clown. Then undiluted fear was induced.

As a six-year-old boy, I was officially introduced to fear. It was a cloudless, beautiful, North Carolina morning in 1973. The day started out routinely as I lunged my way up the school bus steps; I was a little guy with big dreams! Arriving at the elementary school, I bounced out of the bus, kangaroo style, and headed to class with a smile on my face.

Besides lunch, recess was the best part of my schedule. I looked forward to it with enthusiasm. When the recess bell finally rang, my classmates and I eagerly formed a line and marched into the hallway, resembling toy soldiers, where we were joined by other classes ready to release pent-up energy on the playground. Chatter and laughter filled the air as if a rodeo were taking place. I happened to be standing beside an opened janitor's closet. Slowly, I decided to poke my head inside, mimicking a turtle peeking out of its shell.

Unexpectedly, a classmate shoved me inside the closet and slammed the door shut. It was as if I were in the movie *Pitch Black*; I couldn't see a thing. I pressed my palms against the walls in search of a light switch to no avail. I frantically tried to turn the doorknob back and forth, but it wouldn't budge. With all of my might I banged my small fists on the thick, wooden door and screamed, "Let me out! *Let me out!*"

My teacher couldn't hear me. A shiver ran down my spine. I continued to yell and knock, but it was no use.

As the teachers and their students exited the building, the noise in the hallway gradually faded. It was so still you could have heard a pin drop. Distress filled my eyes. I suddenly felt exhausted. I fumbled around in the darkness, located a mop bucket, and took a seat. I could hear the water sloshing forwards and backwards beneath me as its stale odor permeated the chilly air. For a few moments, I imagined that I was the captain of a grand ship.

Then, without warning, the mop bucket began to wobble, as though my magnificent boat were being rocked by stormy seas. I lost my balance and the bucket turned over, landing me on the floor in the murky water.

That's the first time I ever thought of using a swear word.

Momentarily stunned, I slowly crawled toward the door, reached for the knob, and pulled myself to my feet. Fear tears began to well in my eyes and crashed to the ground like water balloons. My little body was so cold that I automatically raised my arms from my sides in hopes that the filthy, bone-chilling water would rapidly drip away. I stood there alone in the darkness, shivering, resembling a rain-soaked scarecrow in the middle of a field.

It wasn't until my teacher had her students line up on the playground to return to the classroom and took a head count that she realized I was missing. She asked if anyone knew where I could be, and no one answered. I can definitely imagine the panic that she was feeling. As my teacher led her students back to the classroom, she noticed liquid oozing from beneath a janitor's closet in the hallway. At the time, that wasn't her main concern; I was. She settled the boys and girls and had another instructor keep an eye on them while she went to look for me. Amid my teacher's search, she approached the closet that was seeping dirty water. I faintly heard her calling my name. I immediately hammered my fists on the door as hard as I could and bellowed, "Help! *Please, help me!*"

She leaned toward the doorframe and shouted, "There you are! Don't worry, I'll be right back."

A few minutes later, she returned with a janitor who unlocked the door. He flipped the light switch, and there I stood, trembling. Blinking my eyes to adjust to the brightness, I slowly emerged with my arms a bit limp but still outstretched. Physically, I was a mess, but that didn't stop my teacher from giving me a hug. Although I was happy to be rescued, I had just met pure fear, and I quickly decided that ruthless emotion was no friend of mine. Apparently, I had been missing for a little over an hour, but fear made me feel as if I had been trapped in the scariest *Scooby-Doo* episode for a lifetime.

CHAPTER THREE

When did you first come face to face with out-and-out fear? Were you worried about a real or an imagined situation? For me, fear proceeded to grow like a climbing vine of poison ivy throughout my life. I realized if I wanted to stop it from taking over, I had to learn ways to control it. I did. You can, too!

I began by exploring my mind in positive ways, and I believe that everyone should delve into his or her own consciousness with the driving force of mental enhancement. To accomplish this, act as if you are in the French city of Paris for the first time. You are happy and eagerly want to explore without limits. The goal: find your strengths whether they are physical or mental.

Next, learn how to utilize them to your advantage. Each instance that you use your strong points, you are helping yourself overcome your weaknesses. You are now learning to medicate yourself from within.

Let me give you some highlights of a talent that I didn't know I had: bodybuilding. At my very first competition, my name was announced to come out on stage. I walked forward, front and center. All eyes were on me. Immediately, fear surfaced, followed by anxiety.

One of the judges leaned toward his microphone and announced, "Show me your quads."

My knees seemed to be locked in place. I grew more nervous. For a split second, I wondered, *Did I train enough? Will I remember all of the poses?* Then I began to tell myself, *You're here now; you can do this. Calm yourself!* I felt my heart rate gradually slow until it seemed in sync with my brain. I took flight as if I were a caged bird finally set free. What a wonderful show!

In the following years, I continued to train to the point that I actually won a number of bodybuilding competitions.

Is fitness one of your strengths, too? Perhaps you have yet to discover the talented guitarist, pianist, drummer, singer, writer, dancer, choreographer, actor, or actress within yourself. Do people compliment your cooking? Your strengths may lie in the kitchen. Do you have a natural aptitude for drawing, painting, carving, or sculpting? Have you always been creative and imaginative? Further explore your artistic abilities.

Are you regularly drawn to one school subject over another? Perhaps you have a knack for mathematics, English, history, or science. If so, this could be a clue to a hidden strength. Explore these areas and their related fields more carefully.

Have you always wanted to learn a foreign language? Give it a try. Does research intrigue you? Are you comfortable navigating electronic devices? Are you fast at typing? These may be some of your assets.

Many times, people are able to take the regions in which they excel and not solely boost their confidence but create livelihoods. That's the icing on the cake. Who doesn't want to do what he or she loves for a living?

When interests you've decided to explore do not come easily, don't be quick to throw in the towel. Making it over the hurdles will cause you to further appreciate your efforts. Even if you ultimately decide that certain objectives are not your strong suits, admit that they were learning experiences. First, you will have gained newfound respect for the people who shine in those realms due to your hands-on knowledge of what's involved. Second, do not conclude that your endeavors into self-discovery were "all for naught." Give yourself an *A* for effort. The processes you underwent tested your perseverance and determination. Guess what? You passed! Those two traits are now among your strengths. Claim them and be proud of yourself.

While on your revelatory quest, don't forget to tap into the everyday character traits that you already possess. Are you a great listener? Can friends trust you to keep their secrets? Do you think before you speak? Are you approachable? Loyal? Conscientious? Honest? Friendly? Is safety a priority? Will you sacrifice to help others? Are you adaptable to new ideas and environments? Are you forgiving? Tolerant? Serious? Humorous? Do you exercise self-control? Can you think on your feet? Are you resilient? Optimistic? Open-minded? Likable? Do people turn to you for advice? Are you courageous? Independent? Mentally mature?

If you answered, "yes" to any of these questions and you are using your traits correctly, they are your precious gemstones. Misuse negates their positivity. Based on your self-knowledge, further investigate the personal qualities that have become common themes in your life. You are bound to uncover some genuine diamonds.

Sometimes, character traits that either you or others have designated as unfavorable can successfully make a turn and sprint to victory in the spirit of a 400-meter Olympic champion. Purposeful redirection of perceived negative qualities can oftentimes be applied into regions where they are both desirable and beneficial. Take into account these three examples:

1. An exceptionally intelligent woman is quite the chatterbox. Every now and then, those in her inner circle are annoyed by her constant verbiage. However, once she channels her gift of gab into public speaking, she comes across as a pro. Regularly after her speaking engagements, audience members will ask her questions, and she is never at a loss for words.

2. In the same respect, a meticulous man frequently goes overboard analyzing and correcting those around him. He is known to be deeply detail oriented. In his twenties, he edited pamphlets and instructional inserts for a manufacturing company. His diligence was highly appreciated. Later, he studied computer coding where his attention to the particulars was essential: one missing or mistyped character could cause his programs to fail. Now he works as an in-demand computer programmer, and his bosses, as well as the company VIPs, think he is a genius.

3. Lastly, a young boy and girl from two different families and cities seem to enjoy arguing with anyone who crosses their paths. Their parents are practically at their wits' end. When the youths

enter high school, they sign up for their respective schools' debate teams. Both of the teens excel, winning individual and team awards. Subsequently, the girl tells her family she's interested in becoming a lawyer. The boy desires a career as a police officer, and eventually, a position in politics. In these scenarios, the youngsters' strong abilities to debate, persuade, negotiate, and argue points optimally work for them.

Can physical characteristics be a source of strength? Outward appearance is where many people center their focus. Why? A vast number of populations, including western society, emphasize its importance. Upon the birth of a baby, most parents immediately count the tiny fingers and toes of their offspring. Not only is the health of their little one a primary concern, but parents also recognize that countless members of their communities automatically form opinions based on what they see. Therefore, if the baby appears normal, that's one less hurdle their little one will have to overcome. Family members and friends instinctively zoom in on a newborn's physical traits, discussing which of the relatives the infant resembles. Oftentimes, total strangers will comment, "What a cute baby!"

As children grow, they learn to brush their teeth,

bathe, comb their hair, and put on clean clothes. However, activities that begin as lessons in basic hygiene are easily turned outward. Kids may hear a parent or guardian insist, "You can't wear that to Grandmother's house," or "Fix that bird's nest on top of your head before the school bus gets here!" Eventually, children understand that certain grooming practices enable them to emerge as presentable in public.

In contemporary societies, as teenagers and young adults interact socially and enter the workforce, they increasingly check their reflections to ensure that they appear as they intend. Doing so can save them from the social embarrassment that generally arises whenever hairstyles are out of whack or visible food remnants are left on clothing, faces, and between teeth. Additionally, people continue to give and receive a myriad of visually based compliments throughout their lives. These kind words could be as small as "Nice eyes" or "Cool shoes!"

Combine these longtime ingrained habits of zeroing in on personal image along with the bombardment of trending advertisements aimed at helping individuals look their best, and it's not at all difficult to comprehend how personal appearance can easily become a focal point.

Are you grateful for the features that you see when you glance into a mirror or after your cellphone's camera rotates to selfie mode? Or are you disappointed? You should always appreciate your appearance, but never cling to it as your primary source of strength. Moreover, ensure that you don't form your distinctive dislikes into the bull's-eye of your mental monologues. Daily doses of self-disapproval are akin to playing a classic game of darts while targeting yourself. Repeatedly throwing arrows of negativity in your own direction will leave your wellbeing with the nicks and indentions of an overused dartboard. Looks are fleeting. Father Time has a way of catching up with everyone. It's best to act as a stockbroker and diversify your portfolio. That way, when one of your investments takes a dive, the others will keep you afloat.

The unearthing of one's interests and innate abilities naturally begins in early childhood. Much of the discovery takes place during playtime. To new parents wanting to fulfill a major instrumental role in helping their little ones tap into their own special strengths: Frequently read to your child whether it's a bedtime fairy tale or a kids' Bible story. Expose him or her to a variety of music, as long as verses are clean. Do you play electronic keyboards, the saxophone, flute, trombone, tuba, accordion, violin, banjo, tambourine, harmonica, or the didgeridoo? Are you an inspiring soprano, alto, or baritone? Do you write songs or literature? Don't be surprised if your tot wants to break out the crayons and try scribbling along on his or her own paper. Share your special gifts and talents with your youngster.

The next time you purchase a small cabinet or shelf unit requiring assembly, allow your kiddo to observe from a safe distance as you put it together. With safety as the top priority, any number of your do-it-yourself projects—from building to cooking—can serve to engage your little one.

As your child develops and becomes a preschooler, visit discount or thrift stores, to keep costs low, and collect a variety of toys in which you believe he or she could show an interest. After you have gathered between five and ten of these objects, arrange them on the floor in front of the little boy or girl. Children are curious. Just because the little whippersnapper grabs an item does not indicate that it is his or her destiny. However, if he or she repeatedly wants to play with the toy piano and medical kit or the microphone and plastic T-ball set, consider allowing the child to further explore these subjects of interest as he or she grows.

Be supportive and nonjudgmental. You are helping your child discover his or her strong points. Remember, parents have major impacts when it comes to encouraging or discouraging their children's interests.

Far too recurringly, scores of people cease to seek their strengths once their educational years are behind them. Keep in mind that humans are ever-changing. Therefore, carve out a little time to bring the wonderfully evolving aspects of yourself to light. When you are open to the possibilities of building upon your previously recognized skill sets and unveiling brand-new ones, they could very well become your passports to a more fulfilling future.

There is absolutely no age limit to personal growth. In fact, many people who have retired enjoy the extra time to pursue fresh, often powerful, ideas. Even those who are far into their golden years have been known to gain newfound joy in working crossword puzzles, reading to children, sewing quilts, making wooden birdhouses, exuding warm welcomes to visitors, and sharing their lifetimes of wisdom with younger generations. Whether you consider yourself a modern piece of art or an ancient artifact, become your own archaeologist by continually excavating the wonders of you.

CHAPTER FOUR

Through the years, I've come to realize that a wide variety of factors can influence to what extent a person experiences fear, as well as his or her ability to handle it effectively. Where does it all begin?

I believe that, for many, it commences prior to birth based on an embryo's genetic predispositions. Additionally, a pregnant woman's choices regarding nutrition, medications, and substances will either favorably or unfavorably impact her offspring. If a mother-to-be is chronically carrying the weight of the world on her shoulders, her elevated angst-inducing hormones are not exclusive to her. She is also subjecting her tiny bun in the oven to her overabundance of cortisol and adrenaline. Reasonable amounts of stress are no cause for alarm, but excessive quantities, regardless of the causes, are bound to adversely affect anyone.

Newborns do not necessarily understand the

vocabulary of the people around them, but they oftentimes absorb the emotions of those in their vicinity as if they were high-grade paper towels. In the presence of a soothing, calm voice, a little baby is prone to coo and smile. Exposed to shouting or an escalating argument, he or she may become fearful and bawl inconsolably.

Children seem to be steel traps for information — especially within the first decade of life. Keenly in tune with their five senses of sight, sound, touch, smell, and taste, they rapidly learn to form basic opinions about themselves and the world around them. Therefore, it is wise to keep a kid's environmental circle as clean as possible during his or her formative years, because parents and guardians are not the only ones with influence.

Each human being is different. Imagine that you and I take four healthy two-year-olds and seat them on the floor, facing one another, in the center of an empty room. We calmly tell them, "Sit still. We'll be right back." Leaving, we slam the door behind us. One child becomes extremely stressed. He cries at the top of his lungs, due to either our noisy exit or his sense of abandonment, or both. The second child is mildly upset, frowning as she glances around the room. The third seems content as she smiles at the others. The fourth youngster finds the "bam" of the closing door quite amusing. He throws his head back and bursts into laughter. Pushing himself to his feet, he pumps his tiny fists in the air and wiggles across the room, demonstrating his best toddler dance. Diversity in genetics, as well as a child's own personal experiences, even at a very young age, can lead to a variation of reactions.

By the time children progress through adolescence into adulthood, they have not only been influenced by their family's values, customs, traditions, morals, beliefs, rules, and household incomes (or the lack thereof), but they have also typically uncovered the expectations of their teachers, peers, friends, bosses, coworkers, boyfriends, girlfriends, or spouses, and of society as a whole. The combination of one's personality, opinions, observations, environment, and encounters can often lead a number of people to emulate the exact behaviors they saw growing up. Many are blind to the connection. Those who suddenly become aware may exclaim, "Oh my goodness! I really am my mother," or "Wow! I've turned into my dad," or " Gee! I'm acting just like my cousin."

Did your father stress about paying his bills every month? Is that secretly why you grow anxious before your next paycheck arrives? Did your grandmother panic when the kitchen pantry was growing bare? Could that play a role in why you buy groceries in bulk and cringe once food spoils, forcing you to throw it out? During tax season, does your mother regularly fret over gathering the necessary documents? Perhaps that is why you find yourself on an annual rant as you search for your own paperwork to meet the tax filing deadline. Was your favorite uncle afraid of being fired if he showed up late for work? Now you panic if you're late for any event.

Learning is part of human nature. It continues throughout life. It's crystal clear that in the process of maturing, young and old alike are known to consciously and unconsciously mimic some of the actions and attitudes of influential individuals in their lives. The first step is to be aware that it happens. Next, closely focus on your behavior—specifically, on what you may have picked up that is unsavory.

For instance, consider how, over the years, you've listened to your best friend repeatedly gripe about being taken for granted at work. Normally, you don't complain, but when you were recently asked about your job, you surprised yourself by defeatedly grumbling, "Man, I'm so unappreciated there."

Do you have a couple of close friends or family members who love to gossip? Ordinarily, you just hear them out, but, increasingly, you've found yourself chiming in, talking about people behind their backs. You may even be displeased with yourself yet unaware of why you are continuing the behavior.

Incorporating some of the wonderful traits that you value in others will not only enhance your life but also the lives of those closest to you. However, taking up a person's less than desirable attributes could set you up for a stressful future. Take inventory of your actions and reactions to ensure that you do not fully embrace another's fears as your own.

By the same token, spending copious amounts of time in front of the television, radio, and computer while zeroing in on the latest news and political reports has the potential to show up in a viewer's, listener's, and reader's moods and attitudes. Televisions are commonly left on inside homes for nothing more than background noise. Regardless of your preferred forms of media, become mindful of the information that you are consuming. Not all reports and images are factual. You do not want to make decisions based on falsehoods. Therefore, don't devour everything that you see, hear, and read hook, line, and sinker. That's tantamount to walking around with a couch half out of your mouth after you attempted to swallow it purely because you saw it.

Beware: results from a steady diet of the shocking, dismal, and disturbing can appear when least expected. Don't allow programing to program you. Oftentimes, going from high-strung toward laid-back is merely a remote control, mouse click, or an "off" button away.

Amid life's journey, it's not uncommon to notice that a loved one or friend displays habits and conduct that you strongly dislike. In fact, you may despise his or her ways so much that you hit the brakes and spin a full 180 degrees, taking the opposite approach for yourself. If that improves your life, fantastic! However, danger may lie ahead. What begins with the best of intentions has been known to pick up the size and speed of a snowball rolling downhill.

Suppose that your childhood playmate's father was never around. You witnessed firsthand your buddy's disappointment. As an adult, your friend vows to be the dad that he never had by always being active in his child's life. How wonderful! Yet, his loyalty to become "Super Dad" causes him to be fired from several jobs for "taking off" too many days. As a result, he's routinely nervous about remaining employed, and his family is invariably filled with angst, wondering if there will be enough money for basic expenses.

Say your parents are ultra conservative. The second you're old enough to move out of their home, you do. Taking a giant leap away from your upbringing, you totally change your lifestyle. You decide to date a person with the reputation of a "wild child." In the beginning, the relationship seems magical. But, when you want to settle down, your "wild child," who is focused on partying and friends, is simply too wild to commit. Your dilemma has you barely able to eat and sleep as your stress level soars higher than the Empire State Building.

Did your mother rarely keep her word? She would say she'd show up at your soccer games but didn't. Did your father agree to take you to the mall but repeatedly changed his mind? Did your aunt, uncle, cousin, or friend promise to attend your graduation but, in his or her typical fashion, never made an appearance? More times than not, you couldn't count on him or her. Therefore, you pledge to go above and beyond, making your word your bond.

On the surface, this sounds like a tremendously admirable policy. Determined to deliver on your promises, you frequently force yourself to attend events and perform tasks out of sheer obligation. In the rush to arrive at the committed hour and minute, you theoretically don your Superman cape while pressing your vehicle's gas pedal to the metal. "Faster than a speeding bullet," you tailgate and zip between automobiles to reach your destination.

It's important to realize that there will be occasions when you must change plans and cannot keep your word. Jeopardizing your sanity and safety, as well as that of others, is overkill. Overcompensating never rights someone else's past wrongs.

Have you experienced a dreadful event? Losing a loved one, enduring a natural disaster, suffering a horrific accident, sustaining a life altering injury, and receiving a troublesome diagnosis broadly activate one's internal alarm system. Due to the accompaniment of powerful emotions, the memories of tragedies are seared in place as though they were raw steaks pressed onto a flaming hot grill, keeping their freshness inside.

It could be that you restlessly recall less eventful situations that didn't go your way. Fixating on disappointments, humiliation, and regrets plants their seeds deeper into your memory. Replaying them, like a looping video, is exactly the water and fertilizer that will ensure their optimal growth. Piling your negative outcomes on top of each other produces a crop of self-doubt, low self-esteem, and habitual overthinking. Add your traumatic events, and your psychological field becomes overrun by the stubborn weeds of negativity. Healthy growth seems nearly impossible.

Some people in our midst fear life itself. Daily twists, turns, and highs and lows periodically leave the most adaptable person rattled. Stress and strain are magnified in individuals who feel they are ill prepared to deal with the inevitable hardships of life. Lacking the necessary tools because they were not taught how to properly handle difficulties or their focus was elsewhere at the time or they consciously chose to dismiss the information, they now stand overwhelmed and petrified in the face of adversity. People in these circumstances repeatedly find themselves on impassioned roller-coaster rides with strong propensities to amp their feelings of anxiousness and fear.

Additionally, a number of individuals fear those whom they do not know or understand. If you subscribe to the mindset that you cannot learn from someone who is different from you, based on that person's nationality, culture, race, creed, social class, or educational level, then you are simply not as intelligent as you think you are. By broadening your horizons and respecting others' differences, you aid the human race as well as yourself.

CHAPTER FIVE

A wesome news: I have discovered that fear only has power if you let it!

Countless individuals become obsessed with the vast array of elements that they believe contributed to their current fears. Understanding the possible reasons is beneficial, but solely focusing on them will leave you drowning in a sea of heartache with more angst on the horizon. It's akin to driving a vehicle forward while staring into the rearview mirror: disaster looms ahead.

Regularly zeroing in on troublesome bygones prompts accusations. Blaming others gets you nowhere. In fact, it holds you back, acting as an excuse for not progressing. If you deem that your unfortunate circumstances are at the hands of someone else, agree to file the information in the back of your memory bank and deal with your current situation. Remember, when you point your finger at another person, three fingers always point directly back at you. They should serve as a reminder: You cannot change the past, but you do have the power to move onward. You can change yourself—in particular, your perspective.

I began developing my self-management skills at an early age. By the time I was twelve, the world's harshness had challenged me for years. Due in large part to my learning difficulties, I oftentimes felt as if I were dropped into the center of a corn maze with no way out. Although I was a child living under my parents' roof, I grew determined to further my abilities to navigate life. I quickly realized that accusing people and blaming my circumstances for my own misgivings would only hold me back. Therefore, I cultivated the habit of taking full responsibility for myself.

Like you, I am a work in progress. Every day presents opportunities to acquire useful knowledge. I am both an eager student and a teacher. Along my journey, I made an eye-opening discovery: I am the founder, CEO, and president of myself.

Think about it. Businesses need chief executive officers, bosses, administrators, and directors— someone in charge of keeping the everyday operations running smoothly. Imagine the ensuing chaos if major corporations didn't have head personnel. When it comes to employment, some job seekers prefer not to take on the responsibilities of being in command. That's strictly a personal choice. However, when it comes to overseeing yourself, there is no option. You are a magnificent, large-scale enterprise. You must step up to the challenge and take on one of life's most critical skills: self-management. If not, you are allowing others—family, friends, and those in society—to do the task for you. In essence, you are reaching inside your head and pulling out your brain, giving anyone who comes along permission to knock it around like a dodge ball.

By depending on other humans' responses to validate aspects of your life, and, in turn, to determine how you feel about yourself, you are gifting your power to them. You're a sitting duck. It's simply a matter of time. Someone is bound to say, do, text, or post something that hurts your feelings. It may even be another's absence of response that has you questioning yourself. Beware: Those who know that you lack personal management skills could take advantage by intentionally manipulating your emotions. Their motives may arise out of spite, revenge, jealousy, or a desire to keep you from advancing attributable to their own quests for control. Have you abandoned yourself? Granting people the extensive authority to tamper with your mind only sets you up for a future full of recurring distress and misery.

Provided that your built-in management skills are

a bit rusty, begin as your own supervisor and work your way up. Do not put the task on the back burner. The earlier you grasp the ability to self-govern, the better. Children and teenagers who have strengthened their mind management skills are less likely to resemble baby birds tumbling to the ground the instant they are nudged from their nests. If you didn't become versed in guiding yourself when you were younger, fear not. You can learn to do so now.

CHAPTER SIX

Life for humankind is comparable to navigating a large sea vessel in the vastness of an ocean. A tranquil, smooth, and brilliant voyage can suddenly turn choppy, restless, and turbulent. Nature itself is unpredictable, let alone if one is attempting to cross shifting waters during a monumental storm. To keep life's colossal waves from engulfing you, train to become the captain of your own ship. Begin taking the helm by understanding the relationship between your mind and body.

Let's get a little scientific. When a rocket reenters our planet, it passes through four primary realms: the atmosphere, hydrosphere, geosphere, and biosphere. Although the four spheres are named separately, they are linked. When a sense of stress, like other emotions, enters a human being, as it invariably will, I believe that it passes through two major, interconnected realms: the mental and the physical.

Picture a hospital patient in need of gallbladder removal. Two physicians, an intern and a general surgery resident, scrub in and enter the operating room. An hour and a half later, the surgical resident has removed the organ, and the intern, assisting all the while, has sutured the incision closed. Together, the two doctors performing different tasks completed the patient's procedure. Similarly, our mental and physical realms, although identified separately, work in tandem to complete us.

To optimize the mental and physical aspects of your being, focus on them separately. This will ensure that they each receive the attention they need, and you will be less likely to trick yourself by using one to indefinitely mask deficiencies in the other. Avoidance and procrastination never serve as substitutes for addressing the real issues.

CHAPTER SEVEN

Since the beginning of civilization, mankind has had a keen interest in human physicality. It is what humans visually take in about themselves as well as others, and, for better or worse, it affects personal opinions and thoughts. In the twenty-first century, many societies seem fixated on outward appearances, so much so that a number of individuals are willing to go to extremes, jeopardizing both their mental and physical health. Don't get caught up in society's pressure cooker. Think for yourself and establish personal boundaries.

As long as you're alive and kicking, give your general health precedence. Drinking plenty of water and consuming nutritious foods better sets you up to take the bungee jump into the further depths of your life. If you are holding on to unhealthy habits, do your best to kick them to the curb. Most people do not eat healthily one hundred percent of the time. However, by doing so more consistently than not, you are upping your odds of coming out on top. Don't be surprised if you notice more pep in your steps. In fact, you could find yourself dancing in the style of singer James Brown or breakdancing like a spring chicken.

As a proponent of annual physicals, I suggest not waiting until something goes wrong to take action. A simple blood pressure reading and routine blood work can reveal any number of current and potential issues. This knowledge can inspire you to incorporate the necessary lifestyle changes required to improve future results.

Is there a hidden biochemical reason your electrical circuits are overloading your emotional outlet box? If, over time, you, or those in your life notice aspects of your personality changing—perhaps you are quick to anger or become agitated and anxious more easily—then chances are that something within your body's chemistry is amiss. Go for a medical checkup to determine if you are dealing with an underlying condition. If you are, seek professional advice regarding the best course of treatment.

Presuming that you've been given the medical go-ahead, avoid a sedentary lifestyle. The benefits of regular activity are numerous and well documented. Movement not only improves the body but also the mind. Because stress hormones, notably cortisol and adrenaline, are reduced and a host of mood-boosting brain chemicals, including endorphins and serotonin, are released, the exerciser experiences a decrease in anxiety as well as an improved outlook. The rise in overall satisfaction could give you the vibe that you're as fit as a fiddle. Keep that in mind the next time you become rather blasé about walking, jogging, swimming, bike riding, or going to the gym. Chances are that once you've completed the activity, you'll be as happy as downhill skier Lindsey Vonn winning a gold medal.

As young children, most of us were hopping with energy. Today, boys and girls continue to run, skip, spin, and turn cartwheels and somersaults. Many pretend to be Power Rangers, Teenage Mutant Ninja Turtles, or leaping prima ballerinas. When permitted to play outdoors, kids rush to their yards, school playgrounds, and neighborhood parks with shrieks of unbridled joy. In the course of a formal education, most eventually learn the true benefits of physical activity in their health and physical education classes. Ironically, that's when some students begin to view exercise as a chore. In due course, their lives become busier, and their athletic shoes of yesteryear are often tossed by the wayside.

If you haven't taken exercise seriously for a while, it's time to dust off your old sneakers and put them on.

Emulating the fitness disciplines of tennis great Serena Williams or wrestler turned actor, "The Rock," is not required to reap rewards. Assuming that you are relatively healthy, begin by introducing more activity into your daily schedule. This could be as simple as choosing the stairs as opposed to an elevator or escalator. Perhaps you will park farther away from stores, forcing yourself to take more steps. If you later want to build upon your accomplishments to develop a more thorough and optimal workout routine, good for you!

Don't forget to change it up. Whether I'm gliding and sliding to my favorite tunes or jogging in preparation to run a race, I enjoy the activities themselves and the benefits of an active lifestyle. If you're prone to burnout, either vary your athletic practices or your methods of training. When you look forward to your undertakings, chances are you'll stick with them over the long term.

Physical exercise doesn't have to be structured or preplanned to be effective. Any exertion that ups the use of your muscles and increases blood flow can aid in improving strength, endurance, and disposition. Challenge yourself. From *A* to *Z*, there are bound to be new activities that fit you to a *T*.

CHAPTER EIGHT

A dequate sleep is of immense importance. It is vital for the human body and mind to function at their best. Are you getting enough shut-eye? Newborns require the most: between fourteen and seventeen hours. However, as one reaches adulthood, essential sleep periods gradually decrease. Between seven and nine hours is ideal for the majority of adults.

Sleep is a biological wonder. While you're in dreamland, your body is as busy as Santa's workshop the week before Christmas. Among the activities are amazing processes: cells are communicating and repairing, energy is being restored, and hormones are released. It stands to reason that when there is a disruption in the sleep cycle, it can easily zap one's energy, decrease mental acuity and creativity, and lower immunity as well as decision-making abilities.

On average, one third of our lives is spent catching

Zs. Make sure you're logging in enough consecutive quality hours, and you will be able to better cope with daily issues. In fact, a huge payoff for those plagued with apprehension is that proper rest decreases the intensity of related symptoms.

Several hours prior to retiring for the night, commit yourself to not dealing with drama. In the same time frame, avoid discussing potentially bothersome topics. With disturbing information fresh in your brainbox, you're apt to lie awake overthinking—tossing and turning with the energy of a laundry dryer—as opposed to relaxing.

The next time you find yourself fighting the urge to hit the sack, think twice. Avoid caffeine, turn off electronic devices, and ensure that your room temperature is as cool as an autumn breeze. Switch off the lights, crawl into your cozy bed, and nestle down. Allow your body and mind to drift away to the land of peace. In the morning, you'll be grateful when you awaken with the zest to take on the day.

CHAPTER NINE

Even if you are taking good care of yourself, you may periodically sense that something within you is out of sync, unusually awkward, or simply off. Have you been excessively emotional lately? Assess yourself.

In some instances, it's easier to pinpoint your feelings and work from there. On other occasions, you will first have to review what you've experienced in order to target the exact emotions, leading to your self-diagnostic conclusion. Either way, you will unearth your core issues. The end results are always worth the effort. Not only will your enhanced self-awareness lead to an elevated ability to quickly and more efficiently help yourself, but it will also provide necessary insight into areas of your personality that you desire to modify. When it comes to your mental irritations and physical indications, detecting the root causes can ultimately lead to answers and solutions.

To begin, think about the troublesome sentiments that you are perceiving. Are any of them disappointment? Anger? Rejection? Jealousy? Anxiety? Dissatisfaction? Fear? Sadness? Embarrassment? Confusion? Nervousness? Shock? Depression? Hopelessness? Guilt? Frustration? Helplessness? Loneliness? Disgust? Sadness? Worry? Stress? Are your emotional symptoms independent or are they accompanied by tension headaches, lethargy, stomachaches, general body aches or other physical manifestations?

Next, discover any correlations between your identified sensations and your recent day-to-day experiences and life events. For example, who did you see today? Did you call someone or talk in person? Were you rejected? Did you leave or retrieve a bothersome voicemail? Have you sent or received an unsettling text or email? Were you insulted or criticized? Are you lacking sleep? Did you start a restrictive diet? Did you overeat? Were you so busy that you missed lunch? Are you taking in too much caffeine? Is there an upcoming test or event that you are dreading? Did you skip your workout? Were you injured? Did you take medicine? Have you forgotten to take a prescribed medication? Are you consuming alcohol or other drugs?

Personalize your inquiries. Become your own detective.

When you take the opportunity to truly focus and ask yourself the right questions, your incredible human brain normally makes the connections. It's similar to hovering an active metal detector along the shore: both the machine's lights and alarm system will automatically engage the instant you happen upon the correct elements. Whether it's as obvious as a school bell practically blasting you from your seat or as subtle as a gentle whisper in your ear, you will instinctively know that you have hit upon the relative issues provoking your distress.

Years ago, I recall feeling as if my stomach were tied into the shape of a pretzel, and I noticed that I was vaguely anxious. These symptoms came and went but endured for several weeks. Why? On the surface, I had no idea. However, after a series of insightful questions, it dawned on me; I had recently been selected to model in my first fashion show. I was over the moon with excitement. Since I felt so confident, I nearly disregarded the notion that the upcoming fashion event could be the catalyst for my uneasiness. After all, I was fully aware of the date, time, and location, and I had cleared my schedule so that there weren't any conflicting engagements.

The fitting and rehearsal went off without a hitch. I was truly grateful to have the job. One of my duties was to model formal attire with a young lady. I was to escort her to the center of the runway, counting the steps in my head, and wave her toward the end of the ramp. Upon her return, we were to perform a touch of ballroom dancing where I would twirl and dip her before exiting.

In spite of my preparation, hidden nervousness was nipping at me as if it were Jack Frost targeting my nose on a cold winter's day. Sure enough, once the fashion show became a page in my history, it was as if a fairy godmother had waved her magic wand over me. My unnerving symptoms magically disappeared.

From that incident, I fully understood that even if a person remains in good spirits, it doesn't mean that he or she is in the clear. Sources of uneasiness often lurk beneath the visible surface as they did for me. Subsequently, I not only decided to better tune into myself in order to spot emotional and physical differences, but I agreed to ask myself pertinent questions to produce honest answers, leading me to tame divergences within my control. When you gain the ability to accurately match your perceptions of discord with the instigating events, you too can begin to choose an appropriate course of action.

Prior to fully wrapping up the inquiries, ask yourself: Am I mentally beating myself up? If so, why? Did I actually do something that I consider to be wrong? If you answer in the affirmative, agree to forgive yourself so that you can move ahead. Otherwise, you're apt to become stuck—much like Winnie the Pooh after lunching on honey at Rabbits house—unable to budge beyond the front door.

Did someone wrong you? Although it may be challenging to enact, make a pact with yourself to let bygones be bygones. That does not mean you should forget the misdeeds altogether. On the contrary, learn from what happened. Take appropriate measures. Sometimes, that means saying nothing and distancing yourself as if the instigator has a common cold. Other times, you may wish to voice the infractions directly to the person. If future circumstances place you back in his or her presence, become your own security guard. Mentally don the uniform. Tell yourself: *I am valuable. Strength resides within me.* By keeping your eyes open, you have the opportunity to get ahead of an escalating situation and protect yourself.

Perhaps, over the years, you have heard countless unfavorable comments about yourself. Nevertheless, you do not have to buy into the sentiments. It is one hundred percent your choice as to how you view yourself. Is your internal narrative telling you that you are brilliant? Stupid? Normal? Defective? Capable? Incapable? Gifted? Lacking? Worthy? Unworthy?

Are you being hard on yourself because you are operating in comparison mode? Does a family member, acquaintance, or coworker have more money, possessions, successes, friends, popularity, and talents? Is hanging around people with grand titles and credentials leaving you with the belief that you're subpar? Did you read online about a young business owner launching his or her own brand? Now you are jealous. Caution: Sour grapes can sour you. Festering envy sprouts bitterness that easily branches into persistent irritability, aggression, and spitefulness. Why subject others to your resurfacing "terrible twos" and yourself to declines in personal growth and productivity?

What is success to you? To each person, it's something different. For some, it's getting dressed or relearning to walk and talk. For others, it's having a close-knit family, routinely volunteering, gaining acceptance into an educational institution, or landing a specific job. The list goes on. Why do you feel inadequate? Are you desperately striving for a life of perfection but conclude that you don't measure up?

Wrong! Quit judging yourself.

No one is faultless. Being flawed simply means that you are a member of the human race and not a programed robot. If, out of admiration, you're honing in on other peoples' jobs, education, expertise, outer appearances, personalities, capabilities, relationships, and accomplishments to the point that you're extremely unhappy with yourself, stop. Chances are that you are comparing what you have titled as "their strengths" against your "self-labeled weaknesses." Are you really being fair to yourself? There are wonderful aspects of you, too. Some are as tiny as a sunflower seed, and others are as big as the giant yellow flower itself. If you have yet to reach your desired potential, don't fret. Be patient with yourself. Everyone is under construction at a different pace.

All human beings have areas of their lives where they excel and where they don't. Before you become fixated with comparisons and consequently bashing yourself, take heed. Not only does one lead to the other, but by repeatedly belittling yourself, you are earning a degree in self-criticism. You're preparing yourself to tackle the world with insecurities and low self-esteem. Is that really the curriculum you want to follow? Understand that what appears to be ideal for one person may not be for another. One size does not fit all. What Sarah does with ease will cause Brianna to struggle. What John can manage, Jared can't. What brings Nadine joy leads Omar to exude bitterness and anger.

Factor in timing. Imagine the following: a towering football player from your county not only played college ball, but he went on to become a first round National Football League draft pick; your brilliant childhood playmate is now the proprietor of a sizeable, successful, expanding company; a striking young girl from your high school landed a professional modeling contract with a prestigious New York agency. You wonder, *Why couldn't something like that happen to me?*

Apart from the hard physical work involved, would you have been ready if it had? When opportunity knocks, some are prepped to open the door, and some are not. Say you were bestowed riches as a young teenager. Given free rein, would you have displayed the maturity, self-discipline, and responsibility required to lead a safe, healthy lifestyle and to save for your future? Age aside, if you are having trouble managing yourself today, what makes you think you could successfully handle fame and fortune or direct a team of employees tomorrow? While you work diligently towards developing a trade, profession, or career, place the same effort into your self-leadership skills. Hence, when you encounter bumps along your path, as we all do, you won't topple over and remain there indefinitely. You will be able to expeditiously get back up and venture forth.

In spite of the initial disappointment when plans are dashed and uncertainty looms ahead, opportunities are actually ripe to enhance intellect and wisdom.

Look for them. Personal growth often comes faster from failure and mistakes than from a steady stream of achievements. Passions for newly found interests and causes frequently arise from adversity. Combined with an optimistic outlook, certain undesired circumstances can subsequently lead one to generate the best possible version of him- or herself. Try turning pain into beauty.

I suggest that you become your own best friend. Be truthful, but don't badger. Envision a longtime pal phoning you every hour or two throughout the day to verbalize what a bozo you are. In short order, you'd be ready to cease all contact. After all, with friends like that, who needs enemies? If you wouldn't put up with others cutting you down on a regular basis, why would you do it to yourself?

Quit self-bullying and become the supportive confidant that you long to have. Foster the relationship; it's vital to bounce back from tough times. Soon you will be landing upright as though you were a wobbly Weeble toy tossed from a young child's hand. In a world full of challenges, if you aren't for you, why would you expect others to be?

Avoid becoming your own "**brain bully**." Harassing yourself for *how you think* takes bullying to another level, and there is no advantage. With a tendency to already be hard on yourself, "brain bullying" adds insult to injury, compounding your problems. If you want to broaden your mental horizons by working on your psyche minus the torment, go for it.

"Brain bullying," although more commonly aimed at oneself, is sometimes directed toward others. Habitually criticizing the way another person thinks won't do either of you good. It is similar to pouring gasoline on a brush fire; sooner, rather than later, it's all bound to go up in flames.

No one wants to be an outcast. However, if popularity is your fundamental focus, you could find yourself on a slippery slope. Acceptance and acknowledgement by school peers, work colleagues, friends, and family members have their perks, but don't sell yourself short. Compromising personal values in order to gain acceptance is not wise. Think twice about the potential and long-term consequences of your actions.

Most know the risks of illegal behavior. Nonetheless, there are plenty of pursuits permitted by law that, in many cases, lead one down a path of struggle, heartache, and misery—not only for the individual but for those with whom he or she is closest. Far too often, what begins as a "fun time" initiates an unintentional pattern that could last a lifetime. Perhaps you have a relative, friend, or significant other who can easily break undesirable routines. Will you be able to do the same?

Are you willing to gamble with your future? Know yourself and your tendencies before leaping aboard the "trying to fit in" train.

If one of your primary goals is to gain favor with everyone who crosses your path, whether you are eight years old or eighty, beware. Stress, disappointment, anxiety, and fear are sure to follow. Why? Pleasing the masses is an unobtainable objective; you will certainly run out of time trying. Helping others through sacrifice and acts of giving are wonderful gifts. Nevertheless, the satisfying, feel-good aspects that oftentimes include recognition, appreciation, and praise, combined with a disdain for rejection, can fuel a person to carry the behavior to extremes. Routinely going out of your way to cater to others at the expense of your own contentment damages your psychological wellbeing.

Maintaining your own peace of mind will enable you to lend a hand to others without overextending yourself to the point that your psyche suffers. Comparable to a flight attendant's instructions regarding a loss of cabin pressure on a commercial airplane, it's most important to secure your own oxygen mask over your nose and mouth prior to assisting another. In the long run, you'll do more good by helping yourself first. Note that even if you have a heart of gold and are as considerate, compassionate, and as helpful as Mother Teresa, some people will never like you; it's simply human nature. The sooner you understand and accept this fact, the better off you will be.

Just as throbbing headaches come and go, so do dilemmas. In addition to life's undesired detours, delays, and sudden, sometimes life-altering changes, also appear radiating sunshine, bright smiles, and cuddly new puppies and kittens.

You can choose to be grateful for what you have or wallow in the misery of belittling yourself. If your desire is to develop an anxiety disorder and live with uneasiness and doubt, go ahead and zoom in on how your glass is only half full. If not, maintain an open mind. Forgo the harsh judgment and condemnation. Anticipate the brilliant sunbeams lurking behind the rainclouds. They always break through. Focus on your journey, not another's, and press ahead.

CHAPTER TEN

Although we humans share basic commonalities, it is apparent that the diversity within our minds is quite vast. Prompted by our temperaments and personal histories, and evidenced by our personalities, we are each unique. Indeed, there are so many variables in the human condition that no two people are affected to the same degree by similar information. Neither will one person perpetually react uniformly.

Here are a few extremes on the spectrum: Some people feel the sting of rejection as if a swarm of bumblebees were viciously attacking them, leaving them to linger in anaphylactic shock. Others speedily trash any refusals without a trace of their existence. When good news is presented, the boundlessly enthusiastic often spring into action, resembling smiling, jumping, bouncing cheerleaders gleefully yelling into megaphones. Whereas those who are undemonstrative may barely, if at all, crack a smile. When frustration and anger sets in, the wildly unconstrained bring to mind a bull in a china shop. Meanwhile, his or her antithesis will, with little effort, appear to be as cool as a cucumber.

Are your actions and reactions blocking you from better days? It's all too easy to get stuck in undesirable patterns. Deep down, human beings are drawn toward routines as if they themselves were powerful magnets dangling near stainless steel refrigerators. When your thoughts and actions elicit an internal tug-of-war and result in self-criticism and nitpicking at others, it's time to reassess. "That's just how I am" is not a legitimate excuse for perpetuating poor behavior; rather, it's a wake-up call to amend.

Some people become frightened at the notion of "turning over a new leaf." However, both young and old must make personal modifications to successfully pilot through the turbulent skies of life. Without making changes, these individuals are basically grounded with very little chance of climbing to their desired altitudes. If by sheer luck they are able to take off, they may circle their intended destinations or remain in indefinite holding patterns until their fuel tanks are exhausted, consequently crashing them to the ground. Clearly, those who successfully ascend tend to do so with great difficulty, or they sooner or later become inhibited by the dense fog of their ways.

Have you zoomed in to evaluate your recent attitudes and conduct? *What am I doing, thinking, and why?* should lead the way. When you recognize that your methods are problematic, you've actually accomplished the first step toward improvement. For your own sake, periodically take inventory. The more self-harmony you're able to achieve, the better for those around you as well.

Are you reluctant because you remain unconvinced that there is sufficient power inside of you to make a U-turn? It's a fact that you have been transforming from the moment of conception—sometimes automatically and, other times, consciously. Take a moment to think back. *You crawled and then walked. You babbled and learned to talk.*

Now, take a brief venture down memory lane. There are bound to be healthy foods that you hated as a child and now you find tolerable—if not absolutely tasty. Back then, you may have claimed that either girls or boys were "yucky," and, as you matured, you obviously changed your mind. Games, hobbies, and even occupations in which you had zero prior interests, may now or in the future top your list of intriguing activities. This is great news! It not only confirms that humans continue to develop as days march on, but it also provides promise for future possibilities. I am convinced that anyone, including you, can favorably transform.

Is your personality aiding or hindering your success? Peer closely inside, and you will attain awareness to further facilitate your understanding and personal growth. Are you ready? Put on your subjective wet suit, flippers, mask, and oxygen tank. It's time to take a fascinating, deeper dive into the depths of your being.

For the following scenarios, imagine two people on their way to work at the same location. One is a "**smooth-wired**" man and the other a "**lightning-wired**" woman. Both are running ten minutes behind. Gender aside, which employee's reaction do you relate to most?

EXAMPLE 1: SMOOTH-WIRED

The instant the smooth-wired man realizes he will be late, he feels as if a stampede of wild horses is running through his body. He begins to perspire. The closer to work he gets, the more he inflates his situation to epic proportions. He visualizes himself walking through the front door only to discover his infuriated boss waiting around the corner with lightning bolts coming out of his ears.

The smooth-wired man envisions himself cowering, imagining he's in an episode of *The Three Stooges* while his boss hammers him with mighty blows of crushing words. Wanting to avoid confrontation at all costs, the smooth-wired man seriously contemplates calling in sick. He knows himself. He will not be able to handle the boss's reprimand. He will dwell on it for days or weeks or possibly even longer, both at work and at home. Analyzing every minute aspect of the exchange, he will wrestle within himself over what he could and should have said and done differently.

EXAMPLE 2: LIGHTNING-WIRED

The moment the lightning-wired woman realizes she will be late she grows concerned. She is certain her boss is going to rant and rave with the gusto of a drill sergeant using a bullhorn. Her temperature immediately soars. However, unlike her smooth-wired coworker, she swiftly concludes, *Let him say something to me, and I'll pop him right in the mouth!* Given the time that it takes her to travel to work, she admits that she wants to keep her job. Therefore, she begins to disarm her raw aggression. She tells herself: *I'm making more out of this than I need to. It's not like I haven't been late for a job before. This isn't the end of the world.*

Although she doesn't look forward to it, the lightning-wired woman is confident that she can handle the boss's wrath. Afterwards, she may periodically ponder the encounter while it's fresh in her mind and she remains in the environment where it took place. However, once she goes home and shares her story with family and friends in the style of a singing telegram, she appears to let it go. Nonetheless, her deep-seated anger lingers on. It generally lies dormant until it's stirred by another memory triggering incident.

Ask yourself: Am I primarily smooth-wired, lightning-wired, or an overall combination of both? To help you accurately answer the question, you'll need more than a snippet of insight. Let's further unravel the smooth-wired and lightning-wired personality types. Keep in mind, both possess traits and characteristics that are considered to be positive as well as negative; it depends on how and when an individual uses them. Balance is the key.

CHAPTER ELEVEN

People with smooth-wired temperaments are among the most caring human beings in the world. In fact, it is their nature to put others before themselves. They are extremely understanding of their fellow humans' misfortunes and challenges. These qualities are displayed in their abilities to easily sympathize and empathize.

As a rule, smooth-wired personality types are thoughtful and eager to help. Even when assistance is not needed, they will offer, "Are you sure there's nothing I can do?" or "I'd be happy to . . ." Many smooth-wired individuals are routinely loyal. Keeping their word is important to them; therefore, more times than not, they can be counted on by others. When it comes to being cast in the spotlight with praise and attention, those who are smoothly wired ordinarily display humility.

However, when situations in life go awry, smooth-wired individuals have a strong propensity to magnify them. They will sharply react to small issues as if they were much larger, and they'll respond with enormous concern. Next, they will look inward for any personal wrongdoing that could have led to the undesired outcome. They tell themselves, *If I had only said this . . . If I hadn't done that . . .* In essence, they host their own mental boxing matches. Now unhappy with themselves, they, easily and often without knowing the real reason why, verbally lash out at those closest to them. For those possessing smooth-wired traits, the endless analyzing, frequent second-guessing, and periodic verbal attacks are standard coping mechanisms.

The mere thought of confrontation can cause smooth-wired individuals to cringe. Why? Because whether they are at fault or not, they know that their overall abilities to handle disputes, insults, criticism, and rejection are not always up to par, let alone if they are targets of shouting. In these cases, their raw sensitive emotions bubble to the surface like a shaken carbonated drink. Controlling their own feelings becomes difficult. If they choke up, appear nervous, or possibly cry, they will embarrass themselves and risk others labeling them as weak. Even if they manage to contain their true emotions at the time, they battle within to do so.

Knowing they are easily and often excessively affected by circumstances and people, those with smooth-wired temperaments have profoundly strong desires to avoid all uncomfortable encounters. Not only will these individuals go out of their way to keep the peace, but they will also go outside their own best interests. They have reputations for being extraordinarily nice, overly polite, and always accommodating. They frequently say, "I'm sorry" and "Excuse me," even when they are not at fault.

Why do smooth-wired people do this? The short answer is that they do not want to dishearten their fellow humans. Why do they care? One reason is because they empathize with others. Smooth-wired people despise receiving mixed signals, negative feedback, and general rudeness, so they usually take extreme measures to extend the opposite. Another reason is that, either consciously or subconsciously, they are aware that any disheartenment they cause can come right back on them. They would rather err on the side of caution by using profuse kindness, than chance accidentally provoking another person. That could escalate the intensity of a situation, placing the smoothly wired person in an uncomfortable, emotionally vulnerable position. Going overboard with hospitality will not keep smooth-wired people from ever experiencing troublesome run-ins, but to them it increases their odds.

In the same sense, given the choice between

disappointing others or themselves, smooth-wired individuals will choose themselves. This is evidenced by their innate tendencies to answer "yes" when asked to take on tasks. Many times, these individuals already have incredibly full schedules, resulting from their lack of saying "no." Regardless, the moment they are asked to take on something new or to help out, they feel surging pressure from the person asking and from themselves.

Smooth-wired people do not like to be put on the spot; this alone can raise tensions. Fear of dealing with the uncertainties of others' personalities kicks in. Therefore, smooth-wired individuals may agree to drive ten miles out of the way to pick up a friend's child every weekday for school, regularly stay after work to tidy the office without extra pay, head a committee, or donate time and money they cannot afford to spare. Later—in many instances, right after they give their word—they may regret their decisions. However, thoughts of disappointing others circle right back around, further locking those who are smooth-wired into their commitments.

Predominately smooth-wired people think more with their hearts, so to speak, instinctively awarding their emotions the title roles. In spite of their warm, nurturing nature, their tender feelings are easily bruised, and they are more susceptible to the pitfalls of their very own doubts, anxieties, and fears. Unbeknownst to the smooth-wired person, he or she oftentimes acquires the reputation of being a worrywart or, worse, a "Debbie or Drew Downer."

CHAPTER TWELVE

D̶o you recognize yourself as someone with a smooth-wired temperament? If you deem yourself to be more than 50 percent smooth-wired, your sensitivities could be affecting your life negatively. Did you know that you can successfully retain the awesome qualities of being smooth-wired while diminishing, if not eliminating, those you do not wish to keep?

1. Face the fact that it is impossible for you to control every aspect of your life.

2. Realize you *can* gain control over your own pessimistic thoughts to a certain extent, depending on what you are experiencing at the time. Right now, dominating the hailstorm in your mind may seem like a monumental task. You may be thinking: *Discouraging thoughts just pop in my head; I can't really control them.* Do not give up!

Imagine this sequence of events: One afternoon, you happen to be strolling through your home with the composure of Smokey the Bear making his way through the forest. You look up and notice a grapefruit-sized water spot on your ceiling. Your jaw immediately drops as you stare upwards lost in a *Twilight Zone* moment.

You decide to investigate by setting up a ladder and climbing onto your roof. Much to your surprise, you find several missing and detached shingles. You reach down, pull back a few, and discover rotting wood. Right away, all the potential consequences of the problem rush into your head: *A heavy rain could flood my house! Termites love rotting wood!*

That night, you dream of floodwater rising up to your counter tops while hyperactive termites wearing red- and white-checkered bibs dine on the rotten wood, annihilating your home.

You awaken early the next morning and spring out of bed, ready to take matters into your own hands. You are on a mission. Full of vim and vigor, you jump into your vehicle and zoom to the local hardware store to purchase the mandatory supplies for repairs. Arriving home, you gather the essentials, throw the wood onto your back with the spirit of a lumberjack, and head directly up the ladder. Atop the roof, you get right to work. You adjust the two-by-fours and nail them in place as well as the plywood decking. Hammering with purpose, you ensure that the nails are perfectly flush with the wood. Thereafter, you complete the remaining steps and top it all off by adding several new shingles, thus solving your problem. You're as proud as Shaquille O' Neil the moment he was inducted into the Basketball Hall of Fame.

Would it have been easier to leave the deteriorating wood and missing shingles? Yes. Would it have been wise to do so? No. When you patched up the roof, should you have pounded the nails in only halfway? No.

Now, imagine aspects of your mental status as the loose, rotting boards in need of repair. Would it be easier not to address the issues? Sure. Would it be wise to do so? No. Should you attempt to make the improvements but fail to follow through? No. Unlike roof reconstruction, you already have the vital, basic tools within to restore yourself. You simply need to know which ones to use as well as when to bring them out and put them to work.

First, it is helpful to know a few of the very basic physiological responses that take place when we human beings experience fear-inducing circumstances. In a nutshell, the initial information is processed at lightning speed by our brains, causing us to perceive the possible threats. Rapid breathing quickly ensues, and simultaneously, our heart rates increase. It doesn't matter if we are being chased by ferocious animals or our own devastating thoughts. The same processes occur. By virtue of having been frightened, all of us have experienced these steps. Remaining cognizant of them can help us to overcome.

Considering that the human brain is the first responder, start by contemplating the situation. Truthfully ask yourself: *Is this a large or small issue?* Your goal is to not make a mountain out of a molehill. Life will present plenty of giants for you to conquer without you creating them. If you react dramatically when the tiniest things do not go your way, you're not only developing a pattern, but you are also causing yourself unnecessary stress.

Just as your physical body requires rest, so, too, does your mind. How, without adequate mental downtime, do you expect to have the energy and clarity to appropriately think and react during a substantial event or an actual crisis? Habitually shifting your cognitive engine into fifth and sixth gear when it should remain in the lower range depletes the necessary stamina, focus, and judgment required for sound decision making. Handling life's colossal blows becomes increasingly difficult. When you are continually living life in the fast lane within, your psyche suffers. Scrambled eggs for a brain have never benefited anyone.

An additional reason not to treat every pebble as if

it were a boulder is to maintain your credibility. Family members and friends won't put much stock in your concerns and stories once they realize you are making "much ado about nothing." By exaggerating, you risk acquiring the reputation of the classic fable character, the boy who cried wolf. In a time of need, you want those closest to you to embrace your worries—not dismiss them due to your tendency to hype things up. Once you conclude that you are not in dire straits, you can and should begin to take charge of yourself.

Picture the following: You are hosting a dinner party tomorrow night at your home. Guests are expecting your famous, rich, homemade spaghetti sauce ladled over *al dente* bird's nests of pasta, topped with a light dusting of shredded sharp parmesan cheese. So, off to your favorite grocery store you go. You grab a shopping cart, pull out your list, and begin checking off ingredients with a pen as you pile your cart sky-high. Much to your surprise, there are no fresh tomatoes. How can you make your famous sauce without them? You ask a stockperson to check in the back. After searching for a few minutes, the employee regretfully informs you, "We won't have any until next week."

As soon as the information registers and you heave that initial sigh of disappointment, catch yourself. It's tempting to feast upon the rejection, dissatisfaction, and resulting inconvenience. *The stockperson didn't check well enough. Now I have to change my whole menu after I spent all this time . . . . Ugh! Wouldn't you know it?*

Instead, immediately try to control your respiration rate in order to reduce your stress and tension. You can do this through deep breathing exercises. To begin, inhale through your nose; briefly hold your breath; and, finally, exhale through your mouth maintaining each of the three steps for 4 to 5 seconds. Repeat the process as needed.

Furthermore, tell yourself, *The information I just received is not a matter of life or death. This is no big deal; it can be fixed.* Next, think of a solution: *I can stop by another grocery store or a farmer's market on the way home.* Adding extra optimism can take you even further: *Maybe I will find an abundance of beautiful tomatoes, plus I can pick up some delicious, mouth-watering breadsticks.*

Now you are turning the situation around. You are learning to deflame and redirect yourself. Your mind and body will thank you.

Since no two scenarios are identical, having a well-stocked, up-to-date, inner-cranial toolbox will help equip you to address matters in a calmer, more mature manner. It is tempting to fall back into old patterns and react impulsively. However, by keeping your thoughts from entering the danger zone, controlling your breathing, and, correspondingly, your heart rate, you will become more adept at rapidly coming to terms with factors beyond your control.

Depending on the circumstances, your thought process may include: *Perhaps I am wrong. I'm overthinking. Maybe I need a minute.* If you are feeling particularly vulnerable, you should take advantage of an opportunity to smoothly walk away and compose yourself. If the break doesn't arise, resolve to stand there and listen. Just because you hear the other person out does not mean that you believe what he or she is saying. If you disagree, you can choose to verbalize your beliefs or not.

Sometimes, remaining silent *is* managing yourself. Other times, speaking up, even though you are scared, is control. No one enjoys that awkward, frog-in-the-throat sensation, but voicing your opinion in spite of your emotions could be in your best interest. Regularly speaking up provides you with the necessary practice so that you are less likely to be shaking in your boots when your voice needs to be heard.

If you tend to fidget when stressed, there are numerous subtle tactics that you can use to relieve tension and quell your nerves.

1. Discretely open and close your fists either at your sides or behind your back.

2. Lightly, slowly, and naturally, pat one or both of

your thighs with an open hand.

3. Spend a few seconds rubbing your palms in a circular motion before clasping them together with your fingers and thumbs. Those in your presence will not know if you are displaying confidence, anxiousness, discomfort, disappointment, or if you are simply thinking.

Your objective is to come up with creative, healthy ways that temporarily distract your mind and relieve uneasiness.

If you have not implemented physical conditioning into your daily routine, I strongly encourage you to clear the possibility with your physician. Upon his or her approval, begin. Regular activity not only improves the body but also the mind. Did you know that both aerobic and anaerobic endeavors are noted to reduce anxiety and elevate mood?

Walking, especially in nature, is a terrific starting point. If you embark with a partner, make sure conversations remain civil and do not evoke Freddy Krueger. Who really wants to deal with a horror character? If need be, set boundaries agreeing not to discuss particular issues. During your outdoor ventures, tune in to the sights and sounds around you. Subject to your environment, listen to the birds' calls and songs.

Observe playful squirrels and take in the majesty and strength of the towering trees in contrast to the tiny, delicate wildflowers beneath. Locate an accessible lake, creek, river, pond, or stream and stroll nearby. A beach is a wonderful setting, too. With each step, feel the sand pressing upward between your toes. Inhale the salty air and tune in to the soothing rhythm of the mighty waves tumbling ashore. Engrossed in the surrounding beauty, both you and your problems will have exited the building.

When there are not enough daylight hours to wander through a park or the length of a nature trail, do not fully abandon the notion. Gear up for an evening stroll. Establish a safe, well-lit area. Remain on the sidewalks, wear reflective clothing, and carry a small flashlight. Glance upwards. Relax as you notice the visible shape of the moon. Witness the sprinkle of stars as they shimmer, mirroring sequins upon the dark, velvet canvas above. On a clear night, familiar constellations are nearly unmistakable. Remember, day or night, beauty lies in all terrains. Don't forget to notice. Mother Nature's wonders are the whipped topping and cherries on top of your outdoor activities.

Yoga is also an excellent choice for smooth-wired individuals because it is a mind and body workout. The popular half moon, eagle, tree, and mountain poses are several that reflect our world beyond four walls. Yoga is known to enhance flexibility, balance, and strength while incorporating breathing techniques and meditation.

Meditation itself assists in redirecting thoughts and promotes mental clarity and tranquility. This alone has numerous benefits. However, embracing the right yoga routine could become a win-win. Countless participants have disclosed reductions in anxiety as well as upswings in relaxation, resulting in improved sleep patterns and lower blood pressure to boot.

In addition to breathing exercises, consistent moderate and high intensity workouts lead to a substantial expansion in lung capacity. The advantages of these exertions are numerous. Typically, there is a boost in oxygen carried to the hemispheres of the brain, resulting in clearer thinking and maximized focus. Furthermore, this chemical element is transported to the heart and other muscles; endurance and stamina are bolstered, and overall lung functions are strengthened. The payoff of an increased ability to catch your breath before others become aware that your jitters are on the rise will certainly heighten your confidence. For individuals whose nerves are inclined to get the best of them, these perks can provide the extra edge needed to dominate one's own reactive patterns in the midst of anxiety-inducing encounters.

Using these basic, helpful methods, customize your

own rescue plan. In the event that your days are already jam-packed, eliminating one or more of your current undertakings will, in the long run, ease your mind by freeing up your time. You are not the animated character Stretch Armstrong. Similar to a rubber band, you can only extend so far without breaking. Prioritize, and then you can reorganize.

Act as your own intermediary. Prepare and follow through using applicable techniques. Don't allow your smooth-wired side to weigh you down as if it were an elephant opposite a mouse on a seesaw. Having a smooth-wired side is fantastic, but not when it's so fostered that it becomes your principal means of operation.

CHAPTER THIRTEEN

Lightning-wired personality types appear to be natural-born leaders. They are frequently referred to as "go-getters," and they don't mind standing up for themselves whether they are right or wrong. In fact, they seem to have an answer for everything. Coaching and coaxing them to handle life's everyday situations is not usually necessary; routinely and almost instinctively, they take the initiative without being told. A firm belief in themselves and their abilities is evidenced by their deep determination to prove the opposite when they are told that they will never be able to achieve something. It's as if their skills, abilities, and dedication shift into overdrive.

Decisiveness is another of their strong suits, especially during emergencies and when time is of the essence. Used constructively, the admirable qualities of lightning-wired individuals are not only beneficial to the possessors but also to members of their inner circles.

More often than not, a lightning-wired person will defend family members and friends when they are challenged and mistreated by outsiders. It's not only notably uncharacteristic, but difficult, for those who are truly lightning-wired to sit idly by while they suspect those with whom they are closest are being manipulated, cheated, disrespected, bullied, or victimized in any way.

To gain a clearer picture, envision the following: Two adults, a brother and sister are discussing her brand-new car. She is inclined to be smooth-wired, and he is chiefly lightning-wired. When the sister tells her brother how her long-awaited vehicle keeps breaking down and that she thinks she was sold a "lemon," her brother quickly and intently raises his head and announces, "Come on! Let's go to the dealership. I'll take care of this for you."

To shed further light on the commonalities of those who are lightning-wired, let's continue to pull back the curtain. Take a look at what is revealed:

Picture a lightning-wired young lady whose ultimate goal is to become a chef in her very own upscale restaurant. She is working toward her four-year culinary arts degree at a large university. All is well until she signs up for business management; the professor has a reputation for making his classes challenging and his exams extraordinarily difficult.

In spite of the overwhelming buzz of her peers who

remain skeptical that she'll make the grade, the chef-in-training buckles down, joins a study group, and puts in more hours learning business management than in any of her other courses. It pays off. She passes. She is one step closer to achieving her utmost pursuit. Instead of withdrawing from the class and completely changing her major or leaving the university, the lightning-wired undergrad became more determined when her fellow students expressed doubt.

Visualize a group of friends eating lunch together. A man unknown by the group strolls by and spews an insult. The predominately lightning-wired members at the gathering will be the first ones to give the stranger a piece of mind in an attempt to set him straight. Although they prefer not to share power, there are occasions when these tough guys and gals will band together.

As long as confrontations remain civil, there is no real harm. However, one of the drawbacks of being lightning-wired is the strong inclination to become excessively aggressive—either verbally, physically, or a combination thereof. This tendency often stems from longstanding, subconscious feelings of being treated unjustly. As a matter of fact, plenty of natural aggressors have been told, "You act as if someone is out to get you!" or "You have a chip on your shoulder."

Bullies are normally lightning-wired. Those in gangs

tend to be as well. In situations such as the previous example of the lunch-gathering friends, outcomes are not always predictable. Focused on themselves and their interests at the time, lightning-wired people's knee-jerk reactions take precedence with little to no thoughts of impending consequences. Depending on who is involved, a heated exchange of words could easily escalate into a fist-flying, hair-yanking danger zone—or worse.

Anytime conditions do not align in the way that lightning-wired individuals prefer, they are inclined to respond spontaneously, assertively, and boldly. They can surge from calm to infuriation in the blink of an eye. In these instances, they may impulsively pound tabletops, desktops, or anything nearby while shouting their disapproval. The sources of their frustrations are endless. Unconstrained, their hot tempers rage. One minute, it could be an uncooperative sewing machine being shoved to the floor, and the next, it might be a fist through a door. From a distance, the chaos may echo that of a toddler beating on pots and pans while screaming out random song lyrics.

Unfortunately, when fueled with anger, lightning-wired individuals do not confine their irrational behavior to themselves. During and after a triggering event, anyone with whom they interact is fair game. At times, innocent bystanders will reap the repercussions.

For example, a lightning-wired young woman and her boyfriend were up all night discussing the future of their relationship. In spite of her efforts, her boyfriend wants out. The following midmorning, the woman drags herself out of bed and goes to work where she serves customers food at a cafeteria-style buffet. The closer it gets to noon the thicker the lunch crowd becomes, and the more the young lady feels increasingly aggravated. She reaches her breaking point when an older man in the line requests not only meatloaf but also extra gravy. She snatches his plate from him and bitterly obliges. As she hurriedly shoves his request back to him, half of the gravy overflows onto his tray. As soon as the man calls it to her attention, she lets out a gruff, "Seriously, man?!! Give me a break!"

Say a lightning-wired man is in need of cash. He drives to a local bank where he has held accounts for years. It's 4:15 pm. While he waits in the drive-thru line for a grueling 40 minutes, he makes a couple of phone calls to vent his frustrations. Finally, it's his turn. A friendly teller greets him. He speedily inserts his completed withdrawal slip, bankcard, and I.D. into the pneumatic tube and presses the send button. A few seconds later, the teller informs him that she cannot dispense that much cash through the drive-thru window, and the bank lobby is now closed.

"You mean to tell me I left work early and lost pay to come here for nothing?" the man quips. Steam is practically whistling from his ears.

He continues to plead his case while she recites bank policies and hours. Fuming, the man speeds away. Arriving home, he tosses his briefcase onto a chair and stomps into the kitchen. He begins to argue with his wife about how to wash the dishes. He is short with his children. In the heat of the moment, the embers of his rage flare. He is not even fully aware that it was the bank incident that ignited his flame.

Bogged down in heavy traffic, lightning-wired drivers are prone to road rage. Whether they are running late or not, they are known to slap their steering wheels, honk their horns, and purposely tailgate the cars directly in front of them while oftentimes going on profanity-laden rants, not to mention if other drivers whip in front of them only to suddenly turn without using the proper signals.

Games, contests, and sports naturally spark competition for all but more so for those who are primarily lightning-wired. These pastimes can prompt their sore loser within to rear its ugly head. Even as spectators of athletic events, lightning-wired enthusiasts are easy to rile. It doesn't matter if they are watching hockey, football, soccer, basketball, baseball, softball, golf, volleyball, tennis, cricket, or rugby; when an official, umpire, or referee makes a call with which they do not agree, those nearby are sure to know.

It's not at all unusual for altercations to commence when quick-tempered people furiously vent their discontent to innocent bystanders and fans of the opposing team. Onlookers may wonder if they are witnessing *Looney Tune's* Yosemite Sam come to life with his "guns a-blazing."

Certain lightning-wired adults have been known to visit bars to have beer fests when their teams lose. Others have temporarily gone dark as though they were Army Green Berets. Some have pressed further, totally veering off the grid for several days or longer. Amid these stints, the lightning-wired do not respond to phone calls, text messages, or emails, and when contact does resume, there had better be no mention of his or her team's loss whatsoever.

Above all, lightning-wired individuals place the highest priority on themselves and their concerns. In spite of their strong desires to defend loved ones from outsiders, it's a very different story when the lightning-wired themselves have beefs with those inside their close-knit circles. Common attitudes are: *You'd better not talk smack to my friends, but I'm allowed to chew them out. Don't you dare fight my siblings, but I sure will. Never talk down to my mom and dad, but I'll do it.*

In the midst of confrontation, these willful individuals often become exceedingly irrational. They stick to their own beliefs like superglue, refusing to accept another's point of view. Regardless of age, children who lash out at the speed of lightning can be especially rough on parents.

Although those who are lightning-wired are distinctly resilient, they never forget the misdeeds done to them. In truth, many pull from these offenses their entire lives. Deep-seated grudges are commonly held against people they know—mere acquaintances and total strangers alike. A number of these strong-willed individuals, including gang members, spend their lifetimes trying to right wrongs by seeking revenge. More times than not, this lifestyle takes a turn for the worse. By dwelling on hate and bitterness, that's exactly what they will exude. In short order, these powerful emotions spill over into the individual's everyday demeanor.

The appropriately directed initiatives and tenacity of chiefly lightning-wired males and females is quite admirable. However, their selfishness, flash tempers, and quarrelsome natures repeatedly get the best of them. They travel an arduous, rocky road. Unconstrained, their futures are at the mercy of their rash behaviors. One impulse away from losing control, they can easily create an eruption characteristic of a volcano. Engulfed in the spewing lava of their own creation, they are painfully transported down the mountain of unintended consequences, subjecting those who dare cross their paths to suffer as well.

CHAPTER FOURTEEN

D o your lightning-wired character traits have the upper hand? You don't have to allow their adverse aspects to reign supreme. Levelheadedness is within your reach. Combine your authoritative knack with the correct knowledge, dedication, and actions. You will triumphantly preserve the pros of being lightning-wired while abating or, better yet, doing away with the cons.

Commence by giving yourself a reality check:

1. You live in the world; you don't own it.

2. Work on ditching the "my way or the highway" attitude. People will not always agree with what you say and do. By and large, bombarding them with hostile words and actions only makes matters worse.

3. Accept that no amount of dominance and aggression will force things to infallibly go your way.

4. Don't think or act as if humanity owes you something.

If you are hard core lightning-wired, in all likelihood you're presently in a state of shock. Facing these harsh realities can leave your mind scrambling. It's akin to clamping jumper cables onto the reverse terminals of a live car battery. The excessive electrical surge will not only induce sparks, but, in a flash, the vehicle may blow a fuse. If you perceive that the same has happened to you, relax. This jaw-dropping information could be the precise jolt that you needed. Now, with your eyes fully open, carry on rewiring yourself.

Introspectively pose the following questions: *Why am I thinking and acting as though a pack of bloodthirsty wolves is chasing me? What really has me so scared? Am I feeling threatened? Why?* As you make your conclusions, recognize that familiarity with how your brain works for and against you is the gateway to transformation. Now, admit that you and you alone are responsible for your own thoughts and subsequent actions and reactions. With that in mind, note:

1. It's not necessary to live every moment of your life fully armored as if you were a knight from the Middle Ages—sword drawn and ready for battle.

2. Although you might not be used to people helping you, be open to the idea.

3. When someone comes to your aid, lay down your weapons. You're allowed to disagree with his or her opinions and advice, but a full defensive coat of armor is over the top.

4. Do not manipulate yourself to believe that certain people are always closed off to your ideas. This type of thinking can result in you jumping the gun—assuming the other person is churning out insults when the two of you are merely having a discussion.

5. Do not label others as "mean" simply because their points of view differ from yours. Ideas and beliefs will naturally vary.

6. If you are at fault for a specific wrongdoing, acknowledge within that you are guilty.

7. Instead of waiting until someone calls you out, voluntarily admit your error and apologize. You will not only showcase your responsibility and maturity, but fessing up on your own terms gives you a handle on the situation.

8. Time permitting, coach yourself. Whether the individual with whom you are interacting is mild mannered or assertive, there is no need to intensify the scene by lashing out. Admit: *I don't like this, but I can keep it from getting worse.*

9. If the opportunity arises, momentarily excuse yourself to a restroom or other quiet location to calm down. This is a prime time to give yourself that short pep talk.

10. When you know that specific people and situations irk you to no end, remain cognizant of these expectations. Right away, you are sufficiently prepared to not allow the individuals and incidents to fully get under your skin.

11. When you find yourself in a dispute, do your best to steer clear of onlookers. Alone, the two of you will be inclined to lower your guards and target the matters of contention without the urgency to use brute force in an attempt to "save face."

12. An opportunity to hash things out doesn't mean the timing is right. As a general rule, never raise a touchy subject with anyone directly after he or she has received bad or devastating news.

13. Since it's impossible to know how much pressure a person is under, respect and reserve the right to suggest tackling an issue at an agreed upon time.

14. Overall, think ahead about the consequences of your words and actions. An apology doesn't always wipe the slate clean. Once some people have seen your "ugly side," they will never fully trust you again.

Ferret out the problematic facets of the ingenious apparatus known as your specific mind. Physically go to a peaceful location. Begin thinking about what makes you angry. Ask yourself: *Is my outrage due to something I'm doing? Is it activated by what I'm failing to do? Does my unhappiness stem from unmet expectations and my self-condemning internal monologue?*

Practice what I've dubbed the "**Four Ps**": *Personalize* your inquiries. *Persist* until you have accurate answers. *Pledge* to change. *Produce* results. Buckling down allows you to get to the nitty-gritty of your issues. Before you know it, you will be able to effectively adjust your unbending thoughts and behaviors as you would your own belt if it were three notches too tight.

Recognize that holding ill will and long-term animosity toward others puts them in control of you. Regularly entertaining people's destructive words and behaviors is an invitation for the sentiments to take up full-time residence where they become toxic. Preoccupied with seething resentment and seeking vengeance, many individuals are unaware that they have forfeited their self-authority. As weeks turn to months and years, many don't notice that it is all a waste of time until it's too late. Even on their deathbeds some remain oblivious.

That's commensurate with a canine chasing its tail: round and round the four-legged creature obsessively runs until it collapses from total exhaustion. Moreover, long after an instigator or foe is six feet under, a number of individuals will remain miffed at him or her to the point that their agitations and deep-seated grudges dominate their waking hours. Never grant anyone permission to haunt you—above all, from beyond the grave.

In the event that your brain resembles a hot-blooded Thoroughbred gone rogue, you must become the jockey riding the horse. Take the reins and redirect the riled animal. Comparably, once you're in your own saddle, you can successfully tame your headstrong ways when day-to-day tensions arise. The next time you're tempted to go eyeball-to-eyeball with someone, apply one or more of the following measures:

1. Execute belly breathing techniques—also known as diaphragmatic breathing. These methods are not only advisable for smooth-wired people, but they are immensely beneficial for those who are lightning-wired. For the 4 – 5 seconds that you sustain each step, envision yourself inhaling calmness, holding it inside, and, finally, exhaling the triggering stress. This can be done on the spot, awarding you an immediate sense of control. Continue the sequence as needed. It decreases muscle tension and can lower

blood pressure. Furthermore, the resulting increase in oxygen is bound to help you think more clearly. Breathing routines can be practiced separately or in conjunction with other tips when practical.

2. In your head, slowly count from 1 – 20, or backwards from 20 – 1, while still listening to your conversational partner. He or she will be "none the wiser."

3. As inconspicuously as possible, gently tilt your head from side to side, giving the impression that you are merely stretching your neck muscles.

4. Implement various standing positions:

    A. Shift your weight from the heels to the balls of your feet and repeat.

    B. Try a pattern of leaning primarily on your right leg and then transferring to your left.

    C. When you are outside wearing shoes, partially bend the knee of your non-supporting leg, and with the sole of the shoe on that foot, increasingly yet casually scuff the ground.

5. Circumstances permitting, quietly pace back and forth.

6. Keep therapeutic stress balls on your work desk at

the office and at home; grasp one with your hand and compress and release as needed.

7. If you carry an ink pen and a clipboard, hold the closed writing instrument upright. With the tip touching the board, slide your fingers down the sides of the pen and methodically flip it on end. This motion can be done on a table or desk as well.

8. Execute static training, otherwise known as isometric exercises: Simply contract a group of muscles for a few seconds. Relax. Replicate or move to another area of the body.

9. Pop a piece of peppermint or cinnamon gum into your mouth. The flooding burst of flavor, along with the mechanical act of chewing, will serve as subtle distractions. To take it further, mentally note the number of times your jaws clench in the process.

By now, you've probably gathered that sequences of low-key, repetitive practices can help you put your genie back in its bottle before it has a chance to grant you an immensely regrettable wish. Strategies that are less structured can be equally effective—particularly when you are already familiar with the controversies at hand.

When you find yourself in these scenarios, recall your favorite foods or complete meals. Contemplations of aromatic home cooking, holiday cuisine, occasional fast foods, and tasty snacks happen to be instantaneous mental soothers. Or reflect on the specific, common activities that you truly cherish. For instance, reading a great magazine, riding the open roads in your car or on your motorcycle, listening to stellar music, baking your grandma's best-loved cookies, watching a preferred TV series, practicing skateboard tricks, tending to your indoor and outdoor plants, cuddling with your purring pet cat, tossing a ball for your dog to fetch, taking a rejuvenating nap, washing and waxing your automobile, chatting with close friends, playing a musical instrument, and spending time with loved ones. Relive the joy, excitement, peacefulness, relaxation, beauty, and wonder.

Practice what I call "**cerebral travel**." Mull over the special, gratifying places that you have already visited. Choose one. Perchance, it's a local, well-stocked fishing hole; a plush, expansive field cloaked in billowing, splendid hues; a flourishing, fragrant, fruit orchard; an enlightening, awe-inspiring museum; or a majestically riveting art gallery. Your select destinations may lie in other towns, cities, states, and countries. Go ahead. Recollect.

Determine your top, future vacation destination. Establish what you'll do. Will you swim with the dolphins in Hawaii? Explore one of Walt Disney's theme parks? Photograph lions, elephants, giraffes, and hyenas while on safari in the African savanna? Ride a camel near the ancient, mystical pyramids of Egypt? Ski or snowboard down the pristine, white-blanketed slopes of the Swiss Alps? Take in the prospective views, scents, sounds, and sensations. Whether you're reflecting on an actual excursion, or you are wishfully imagining, "cerebral travel" is a no-cost, effective method to ease you through the first leg of your itinerary.

On your expedition to become less reactive and more intentional, you'll discover an array of enjoyable, advantageous practices. I suggest that you incorporate a few of them into your lifestyle. For the well and able-bodied, high-intensity, exertive training is an effective way to release pent-up frustrations and keep new ones at bay. Aside from conventional pursuits, it's fun to experiment with new concepts.

My idea of "**sand throwing**" is an excellent place to start. All you need is a small beach pail, a strong back, and, of course, access to sand. An oceanfront or seashore is perfect. With both hands on your plastic bucket, one on the lip and the other bracing the bottom, bend, and scoop to fill it. Stand upright. Moving parallel to the water, take a few steps and forcefully heave the multitude of tiny, collected grains out in front of you. Simultaneously and symbolically release your frustrations into the heavens above. Repetition makes for an energy-intensive yet restorative venture. Switch hand positions to even the drill. To up the exertion, scoop heavy, wet sand. In the event that your natural environment is not conducive to throwing sand, try the same procedure in an open area using snow, leaves, pebbles, or dirt.

Have you thought about taking traditionally indoor activities out into the open air? Since natural scenery promotes tranquility, it makes sense to pursue physical training outside whenever possible. For example, instead of habitually running on a treadmill, jog lakeside, in a public park, or on a vast, open track. From time to time, ditch the stair stepper and the indoor rock wall in favor of outdoor hiking and mountain climbing, respectively. In lieu of taking a whirl on a stationary bicycle that's enclosed by four walls, move the machine onto a patio, balcony, porch, or under a gazebo. Even better, go for the real deal. Pedal down a breezy, secure, and challenging pathway or grab a buddy and your helmets for an afternoon of mountain biking.

Boxing's jabs, hooks, crosses, uppercuts, and roundhouses are not limited to fully enclosed buildings such as gyms. Alternatively, use a stand-up punching bag to pound some out-of-door rounds. Based on where you live, you may or may not be able to locate an outdoor aerobics class. If not, go solo or recruit a few friends.

While you're at it, intermix boxing moves for a vigorous, immensely satisfying routine of box aerobics. Personally, I love to dance—especially outside.

In my adulthood, I began regularly visiting a community beach in Pensacola, Florida. Dressed in comfortable clothes and a pair of supportive, bright, ivory-colored sneakers, I would briskly walk the length of the wooden pier toward the approximately 12' x 12' platform overlooking the bay. What a breathtaking sight! In the background bobbed vividly colored sailboats. In the foreground were generally smaller fishing boats, catamarans, and, occasionally, jet skis. For years, I would routinely adjust my trusty headset that was attached to either my vintage portable AM/FM radio or my newfangled iPod, and I would move and groove between the four corners of my outdoor stage for hours.

Consequently, my peripheral vision became quite keen. In fact, it saved me on more than one occasion from waltzing and free-styling right into the choppy waters below. The spirited little marine creatures within my field of vision often fueled my imagination. Were the vibrations of my dance moves beckoning them to join in? Dressed in their opalescent, glittering costumes, the fish made superior backup dancers. They'd jump, flip, skip, and slide across the caps of the inlet. In the shallows, I observed the blue-tinged crabs, and they could not only shake a leg. In full animation, they'd sway back and forth, pincers snapping in the air, keeping perfect time with my beats.

Usually, before I departed the pier, I'd face the bay with outstretched arms. Inhaling thoroughly, I would take in the essence of my surroundings, and then I'd close my eyes and complete my breathing exercises. Sometimes the exhilarating breeze was warm, and the sunshine seemed to kiss my face. Other times, the wind's gusts were invigoratingly cool or outright cold. Now and again, delicate raindrops would mist from the clouds miles above. On occasion, the droplets grew in size and intensity. They resembled a troupe of clog dancers on top of my head, leading me to make a mad dash through the parking lot to seek shelter inside my car.

Come rain or shine, my outdoor dance sessions invariably left me with elevated perceptions of freedom, accomplishment, and renewal. For me, it has been therapeutic. Try it. It may be the same for you.

CHAPTER FIFTEEN

Whether your feelings are easily hurt—even when no one is intending to do so, or you fly off the handle—often unprovoked, your emotions are calling the shots. No one can become assuredly content while dominated by sadness, tears, and uncertainty or by rage, aggression, and grudges. It's comparable to playing the arcade game *Whac-A-Mole*: once the large mallet whacks a mole back into its underground hole, more of the pesky little critters unfailingly pop up.

Are you disproportionately wired? If so, you could be a ticking time bomb ("**TTB**"). Commonly, TTBs are disasters waiting to happen: These individuals seem to wait with bated breath for someone to disagree with them or for something to go wrong so that they can, "legitimately," explode. It's a way for them to release steam at another's expense.

Smooth-wired personalities prefer to unleash on their

fathers, mothers, siblings, children—whoever is within their close-knit circles. Lightning-wired individuals will blazingly react in full blast with little to no thought about the aftereffects, making anyone and everyone fair prey. Commonly, both the smooth- and lightning-wired are unaware that they have become TTBs until others bring it to their attention, potentially setting off more explosions.

Have your nearest and dearest advised you to improve aspects of your personality? It's easy for smooth- and lightning-wired individuals to receive well-meaning, personal recommendations as kicks in the teeth while perceiving the advisors as the ones with the real problems. As a result, the heartfelt concerns and suggestions of those who care are typically dismissed. If you notice a recurring theme being voiced to you about yourself from trustworthy sources, it's time to look into it.

Note that accurately assessing your behaviors from the inside out is sometimes difficult, whereas the view of revered family and friends could be crystal clear. Therefore, the next time you are offered constructive criticism, be open to the idea. It can't kill you. Everyone has areas in which they could and should improve. Listen carefully. Resist the inclination to fight or cry. What you hear could be eye-opening. When you discover validity in the information, look upon it as a pivotal building block to create an improved and exemplary you.

A number of smooth- and lightning-wired individuals believe they cannot successfully solve their problems unless they are upset, scared, or angry. Some claim that amplifying passion and drama indicates how very deeply they care. Showcasing intensity via panic and hostility does zero to support a situation. It typically causes smoldering difficulties to combust. A fired-up tone of voice and demeanor easily spark the same in those engaged in direct communication as well as in others nearby. In seconds flat, the impassioned woman or man is apt to be arguing with everyone in sight. Is this you? Remain calm. Maintaining your composure allows you to formulate rational answers more quickly and efficiently without exasperating the person who is willing to discuss your concerns.

In present-day society, innumerable people are overwhelmingly preoccupied with how to fix everyone else. Temperamental people are prone to this to a greater extent. They progressively bandage their own minds by busying themselves. They concentrate on people, places, things, and actions as though they were pulling ideas from a mixed bag of nouns and verbs. Some turn to substance abuse. Many keep up these patterns their entire lives—never centering on their core matters. Don't get caught up to the point where you have to be doing something nonstop in order to live with yourself. That's merely sweeping your issues under the rug while creating a bigger, future dilemma. Is an ostrich with its head in the sand really hidden from a cheetah? No. The swift cat will effortlessly pounce on the large, flightless bird, and then the feline's dinner is served. If you try to avoid your problems by burying your head in the sand, don't be surprised when the truth bites you.

There are instances where ultrasensitive individuals and those who are thick-skinned may purposely procrastinate or altogether avoid their responsibilities to call, text, email, and meet another in person. Why? It's not because they're being lazy. Rather, it's on the grounds that they've had time to put on their thinking caps, and they sense unfavorable outcomes for themselves. In cases where they know the individuals, they may choose to delay or avoid reaching out due to the other person's antagonizing, mean, manipulative, and disrespectful ways.

Given these circumstances, suspicions of confrontation and rejection immediately take up residence in the overthinking, tenderhearted person. In contrast, with nothing to personally gain, the impatient and fiery individual sees no need to bother. When both the smooth-wired and lightning-wired are unfamiliar with whom they need to contact, their curiosity may prod them to reach out; nevertheless, fear of the unknown could provoke hesitation. Despite the different reasons for their actions, one thing is definite: their emotional pots of gumbo are already filled to the brim. The addition of one extra undesired ingredient or the slightest agitation will directly turn up the heat, causing their strong feelings to overflow.

Another commonality shared by distinctly smooth-wired and lightning-wired individuals is that those closest to them are never fully at ease in their presence. Knowing they are easily offended, family and friends will repeatedly tiptoe around certain topics in order to avoid prompting tumultuous reactions. In spite of the careful efforts of those who are attempting to keep the peace, the ability to do so is uncertain and can prove to be an exhausting, uphill climb. Do you really want people wishing to avoid you, dreading your phone calls, and immediately walking on eggshells the instant that you appear?

It's often trying for smooth-wired and lightning-wired people to relate to one another's behavioral extremes. Snapped up in a firecracker of offensive verbiage, an incredibly nice person may wilt like lettuce leaves abandoned in a hot car for hours. He or she is at high risk of being walked upon. On the other hand, an ill-tempered individual who reacts at the speed of lightning may find it nearly impossible to bite his or her tongue. He or she is liable to struggle with showing compassion when situations require it.

Fortunately, rooted inside—either deeply or near the surface—both groups have what it takes to dust off the errors of their old ways and polish themselves up as new. Whether you are fundamentally smooth-wired or lightning-wired, it is time to unlock the vault between your ears to bring forth your key, priceless, overlooked jewels. These invaluable beauties not only include kindness, love, loyalty, respect, patience, caring, restraint, flexibility, peacefulness, agreeableness, and understanding but also sternness, resistance, harshness, indifference, aggression, and the ability to project these traits utilizing the appropriate sincerity, compassion, and unwavering authority required.

Everyone needs these qualities and many more. Although you may hope to never use some of them, they are all vital to possess. They will help you create a healthy balance. That way, you can reach into your mental treasure chest and pull out enough of what you need at the time based on the person with whom you are interacting. Do not confuse and misuse. Because someone shouts, punches, or mistreats you does not mean that you should give him or her an equal dose of the same.

Since no two people are wired explicitly alike, study the beneficial tips listed in the previous chapters under the categories of smooth-wired and lightning-wired and interchange them as desired. Customize a plan that works optimally for you.

Furthermore, become mindful of your ways sans self-criticism. Write down what you want to work on. Doing so breathes life into your thoughts. A notebook, journal, cell phone, or even a piece of paper carried in your pocket or wallet works. Post sticky notes where you will see them both morning and night. If you don't have a vision board, consider purchasing or making one. A cork bulletin board; a thin, flat piece of wood; or an extra-large picture frame with thick backing and no glass will do the trick along with a small box of pushpins. In addition to photos, referencing tangibles, and inspirational words, don't forget to add your psychological aspirations—they are the most important of all.

In fact, everyone can benefit from what I call a "**brain board**." It's smaller than a vision board and is focused strictly on a person's mental health. On it, plainly state your personal psychological goals. Include the "how-tos." Affix encouraging quotes as well as pictures. Perhaps a snapshot of a spectacular orange, pink, and blue-skied sunset will boost your mood. The slightest improvements should be jotted down and pinned up as future motivation. This forthright, interactive approach can distinctly aid in reaching your innermost objectives.

Increasingly live with an attitude of gratitude. Are you able to see, hear, and read the words on this page? There are people who cannot. Are you capable of walking, running, and brushing your own teeth? Consider yourself blessed. Don't waste your hours rehashing the missteps of the past and complaining and feeling sorry for yourself. The same time and energy can be used to productively live and enjoy your life while constructing a brighter future.

Cultivate the daily habit of writing, thinking, and verbalizing your appreciations. You will soon discover distinct advantages. These include not purely an enriched appreciation of life's pleasures but a strengthened grip on handling adversity as well. It's as though one of Major League Baseball's greats—Hank Aaron, "Babe" Ruth, or Willie Mays—has joined your team. With a hard hitter stepping up to the plate and going to bat for you, your odds of winning a World Series just multiplied tenfold.

Some people prefer to incorporate gratitude into their prayers. The decision is yours. If you choose to do so, then humble yourself and graciously ask God for the comforting desires of your heart and state the things for which you are thankful. Praying prompts hope, faith, and belief. All three elements are of great importance.

A person filled with hopelessness is convinced that he or she has nothing. In the absence of extreme caution, self-destruction is right around the corner; it's plainly a matter of time. Although troubles will clearly arise, never delete hope. Without it, fear takes over and completely rules. Are you breathing? Then there is always hope for a better tomorrow. Have faith in yourself. Remember the successes you've accomplished, whether small or large, as well as the good fortune that has befallen you from out of the blue. You did not reach your current age without some things going right. Trust this fact.

Now, place the following statement inside of you and believe: *I have, I can, I will*. Recite this compelling *past-present-future* affirmation and follow it up with action.

You are on your way to obtaining the required balance that improves every aspect of your being. Before you know it, secure control of your disposition will be firmly in the palms of your hands. Prepare yourself for increased self-esteem, and, in turn, confidence—in addition to a rise in contentment with others. In due course, you will no longer recognize yourself as primarily smooth-wired or lightning-wired. Possessing equal proportions of both, you will have graduated to become a "**smooth-lightning-wired**" person.

Congratulations! Now, look at yourself in the mirror. You are "**smooth-lightning**." It's as cool as it sounds, and it can be yours.

CHAPTER SIXTEEN

Too many people believe they will reach a state of ultimate contentment once they've acquired more of their worldly desires. They base success and happiness on who and what they have. However, without the inner balance that brings peace, this type of satisfaction is fleeting.

These individuals, from all backgrounds and educational levels, seem to travel endlessly on the hamster wheels of life. When they do pause to glance into their innermost mirrors, they dislike what is revealed. Either their true character or something that they believe makes them "less than" compels them to leap right back onto their running wheels. It's an endless cycle. Just like wheel-addicted hamsters, they're going nowhere fast.

To try to avoid this behavior, one of the best things parents can do is teach their children, by example, to work favorably on their mental health. That way, the kids' bodies won't far outgrow their minds. This safely puts the youngsters in their own driver's seats—in a manner of speaking. Early on, little ones will quickly realize that they are ultimately responsible for themselves and their attitudes. Promising outcomes are not ironclad, but chances increase when moms and dads lead in positive ways.

For instance, one morning, a woman gathers her three youngsters to drive them to a local elementary school. Outside, with kids in tow, she notices one of her front tires is as flat as the pancakes her munchkins scarfed down for breakfast. She kicks the deflated rubber treads while a few curse words spew from her mouth. Whether she knows it or not, she's coaching her offspring to do the same.

Ten miles away, a similar scenario is playing out with a father and his brood. However, he is much calmer. He bends down to examine the tire and states, "We didn't need this, but things happen. We will deal with it." He, too, is training his kids.

In the first scenario the mother's message is: *Act foolish and immature when things go awry.* If the negative behavior is repeated and a child emulates and pulls from it throughout life, in all likelihood he or she will experience unnecessary difficulties with others— regardless if it's at home with parents, in school, at work, or in personal relationships. By contrast, the parent in the second scene, in this case a father, communicates: *Composure and maturity lead to problem solving.* He is productively contributing to his children's mental states.

Perchance you or someone you know is an adult, but, in many respects, acts and reacts like a child. Clearly, physical maturity does not automatically bring mental maturity. Neither does basic or higher education. Advanced courses of study are wonderful and powerful. However, there are plenty of people with associate, bachelor's, master's, and doctoral degrees who have never fully entered the driver's seats of their minds. At first glance they appear to have it all, but do they really? In society, they ride on their credentials; however, between their ears, for one reason or another, there may live personal dissatisfaction and turmoil. Their inner frustrations sway their outlooks. Sooner or later, their discontent becomes evident either to their family members, coworkers, or complete strangers. Arguing vehemently over things that seem minor, such as a pair of shoes or who said what when, can be a sign of their separate, underlying issues.

In summary:

When a lovely-looking house is built on shaky ground, it only takes a minor jolt from the earth to induce crumbling.

Following one shake of an overripe apple tree,
the fruit drops in droves and begins tumbling.
If you were leaning against the dwelling or standing
beneath the tree,
in the midst of the situation, you'd certainly wish to flee.

And so it is when others experience one's personal wrath. No one wants to be pummeled by boards and bricks, apples, nasty words, and more. Your mind is your foundation. Make it stable. It will bear fruit. What kind it is will be up to you. If your head is exceedingly ripe with self-disappointment, anger, and regret, it's time to bring out your pruning shears and use them.

Are you a "**mental hoarder**"? It's someone who, in addition to the everyday, normal data, gathers and accumulates tainted information about themselves and others. What these compilers do with their findings varies. They either feed their innermost voices, disapproving of their perceived flaws, or they aim outward, criticizing others as a way to boost their own self-esteem. Most mental hoarders practice a combination of both. Eventually, they become buried alive in their stockpiles of negativity. When more important information comes along, they may have difficulty grasping all of it because they have yet to declutter their brains.

Did you know that chronic negativity generates fear? It's true. The sheer number of individuals who entertain negative thoughts is mentally boggling; many do so without realizing that their focus on these inflammatory sentiments culminates in bouts of uncontrollable uneasiness, dread, distress, and alarm. Furthermore, this mindset prompts unfavorable presumptions of future outcomes. Don't manifest what I call the "**monster of ill speculation**." By welcoming and breathing life into it, you're giving it legs to run amuck.

Are you at least 50 percent optimistic? Or are you far too pessimistic for your own good? Find out. Several times a day over as many days, take a few minutes to notice what's truly on your mind. What topics are you cognitively and verbally initiating? When others introduce subjects, what aspects are you chiming into and elaborating on? If your answers sound more like the tail end of the western film title *The Good, the Bad and the Ugly*, acknowledge the reality. Recognize that you do not have to permit criticism and judgment to rule your psyche. Nor do you have to allow unfavorable bygones to haunt you as though you were Ebenezer Scrooge being led by the Ghost of Christmas Past.

As confirmation that you're going forth, initially make a mental list of what has you frightened to the point that it's holding you back. It could be that you've experienced a broken relationship. Maybe you're blaming yourself for an accident. Or, quite possibly, one or more of your endeavors have been unsuccessful. Do you possess a trait or uniqueness that you consider embarrassing? Do you have an internal or external condition, disability, or disorder that you believe others view as a weakness?

Using sticky notes or small pieces of paper and a pen, jot down each drawback separately. Then, head outdoors. Implementing a small garden shovel, dig a hole in the ground. Insert each documented difficulty into the hole one at a time. Now, cover them with dirt.

If you prefer not to write your plights or conditions, place your clenched fist in front of your mouth as if you're about to chough. Whisper your worries, one at a time, into the circular opening of your fist. Representatively, drop each secret into the hole that you have unearthed. Next, bury those parts of your past beneath the soil. By acknowledging them and giving them an official burial, you'll be less likely to cling to them when future circumstances rouse the entombed memories.

If you'd rather cremate them, safely insert them into a fireplace or bonfire. Using the clenched fist method, you can opt to symbolically release each of your setbacks toward the flickering flames. These methods can actually benefit anyone desiring to distance him- or herself from previously unpleasant, hurtful, and tragic events.

LIKEWISE & VELVET SKIES

What you feed your mind is as far-reaching as what you feed your body, if not more so. Envision this: You have stockpiled cans of beans in your refrigerator, freezer, kitchen cabinets, and pantry. The next time that you open one of the doors as well as thereafter, beans are all that you will see and retrieve. Similarly, if you stock your brain with negativity, that's what you will pull out every time—*I'm not good enough, I've failed, He's so mean, She thinks she's all that and a bag of chips, I hate my . . ..*

Interestingly, this same analogy applies to the person with a beautiful dream kitchen or a humble basic one, or an individual totally without who is toting a can or two of beans in a plastic bag. In other words, social standing and income have nothing to do with it; what you store is what you'll get.

Are you spending more energy than you'd prefer complaining? If so, you may have developed what I refer to as a notoriously "**negative noggin.**" If you tend to find fault with people, allowing little room for human error, and you dwell and elaborate on your dissatisfactions, rarely detecting good unless prompted by another—plus you have an "I can't" attitude—then you have become a "negative noggin."

When, on the other hand, you are often willing to make allowances for others' errors, and you frequently contemplate and voice your overall satisfaction and joy in spite of your adversities, and your "I can" mentality enables you to encourage others, then you are what I refer to as a primarily "**positive processor.**"

A person who doesn't look for joy will never find it. Do you take to bad news like a child does to candy? Breeding discouragement, bitterness, and unhappiness blocks encouragement, positivity, and enrichment. Don't become a "negative noggin." If you already have, nix it.

How? Employ what you have learned within these pages. It's all part of my "**mental health diet for strength and immunity.**" You are going to become skilled at stocking your mental pantry, cabinets, refrigerator, and freezer with positive thoughts about yourself and the world around you. In essence, your "negative noggin" will soon transform into a more "positive processor." Then, when you trip and fall—as we all do—you'll bounce back as though you were a professional gymnast on a trampoline.

Knowledge of what is commonplace will better prepare you to repeatedly and hardily endure, especially when the circumstances and outcomes are less than desirable. Check yourself:

1. You do not have all of the answers to why others behave as they do. Let's say that your friend has not returned your phone call. He normally does,

so you instinctively assume he's mad at you. Realistically, he could have been busy. He may have forgotten to charge his cell phone. Perchance he left it at home or in his car. Maybe he had a work deadline, prompting him to mute the volume or completely turn off the device. Perhaps he really *is* upset with you. Is our planet going to implode? No, and neither should you.

2. Everything and everyone will never be one hundred percent as you desire. No one relishes a disruption of plans or the added difficulties of the uncooperative. In those events, frustration and disappointment naturally ensue. However, accepting that hiccups will occur even in well-orchestrated initiatives has a way of decreasing the extent and duration of the accompanying aggravation.

3. Face the fact that you will make brilliant as well as poor decisions, and that some cannot be changed. Instead of rubbing salt in the wound by trying to rectify an impossible situation, learn from it and march forward.

4. With whom are you spending the majority of your waking hours? "Negative noggins?" Intensely dismal perspectives, especially over the long haul, seem to be contagious. Guard your mind. Feed the

pessimists out of long-handled spoons whenever possible. If people that you love fall into this category, you will have the knowledge to help them if they so desire; plus, you can lead by example. In the meantime, resolve to add "positive processors" to your circle of acquaintances and friends to better balance the scales.

5. How do you react when the going gets tough? Your response is telling of your current character and can reveal areas that need work. It could be that while all is well, you are "Mr. Pleasant" or "Ms. Delightful." However, when circumstances are contrary, so are you. Agitated "Mr. Pleasants" and perturbed "Ms. Delightfuls" have been known to suddenly spin into fits of rage resembling the character of Taz, the Tasmanian Devil.

Visualize the closing night of a Broadway production where the lead actor delivers the performance of a lifetime. As the cast takes its final bows, the audience imparts a ten-minute standing ovation. Among the whistles and cheers, roses are tossed onto the stage in appreciation. It's easy for the entertainers and production crew to graciously smile while they are being praised. On the flip side, how would they react if a rowdy, upset crowd booed and barraged them with insults and rotten tomatoes? Naturally, they would not be as receptive. The bigger question is *Would the cast and crew members allow those disappointingly sour moments to contaminate their hours, days, months, and years to come?* Their decisions lie in their heads.

6. When you recall your former regrets and embarrassments, do they motivate you to progress toward improved objectives, or do they leave you bleak and stuck in a rut? More often than not, this type of rehashing is better left for trashing. If it is not empowering you to take constructive action, you do not need it. Whining doesn't change things, *doing* does.

A major component of my previously mentioned mental health diet is to ensure that your internal storage shelves are stocked with plenty of leafy-green positivity. Take this gradual, yet quick and effective approach:

The next time old patterns of criticizing something or someone—including yourself—pop into your head or out of your mouth, only allow yourself to indulge in three negative statements followed by a fourth that must be positive. This forces you to begin thinking as a "positive processor." Continue decreasing the negatives to two and then one, always followed by a positive. Eventually, there will be occasions when you can eliminate pondering or voicing anything that's discrediting. For easy reference, I have labeled this my **"3-2-1 positive reinforcement approach**." To enhance motivation, remind yourself of the old adage that many of our grandmothers and mothers taught: "If you're not going to say something nice, don't say anything at all." It's applicable to your internal narrative as well.

Unaccustomed to holding yourself accountable for your nay-sayings, your biggest hurdle may be catching yourself before you've gone too far. As though you are playing the childhood game, "Red Light, Green Light," you will have to initially freeze noncompliant, harmful thoughts and spoken words in their tracks with a resounding inner shout of "Red light!" If they keep coming, send them back to the starting line. My "**red-light technique**" can be used to disrupt any intrusive thoughts.

Fortunately, there are various subtle and effective ways to remind yourself of your new program that won't alert the masses. Options can be combined and include the following:

1. Purchase a sheet of small, identical stickers. They can be as simple as plain circles or more elaborate. Place one decal each on your bathroom mirror,

cell phone, and computer. Consider adding one inside your vehicle, on a notebook, to the top of your work or study desk, and on the outer surface of your favorite coffee mug or teacup. With a mere glance, the stickers will serve as reminders for you to stick with your plan.

2. Wear a positivity ring or bracelet. Purchase an inexpensive wristband or silicone ring and designate it for that purpose. If you want something cheaper, encompass your wrist in a colorful, loose-fitting rubber band. If price is not a concern, go for a piece of costume jewelry or something much nicer. The point is to associate the new jewelry with your venture toward positivity. Each time that you gaze at the adornment encircling your wrist or finger, you will instantly reaffirm your engagement to self-improvement.

The more optimistic your prevailing perspective, the better you will be able to endure adversity without crumbling under its pressure.

Do you sometimes feel as though your get-up-and-go got up and went? Even a jaundiced eye can see through rose-colored glasses. A bright outlook fuels motivation to succeed.

Are there tangible objectives you've yet to achieve?

Do you have a "to-do list" a mile long? Commence by prioritizing your goals, listing them from the smallest to the largest. Check them off as you conquer them. Printing them for visibility enhances a sense of mastery. After completing the very first undertaking, your self-respect will climb. This elevation is an energy source. Use it to carry through with your second task, further boosting your self-esteem. Continue the pattern at a reasonable pace. You're on your way to becoming a *doer* as opposed to merely a *talker* and *wisher*. Stick with the method, and *doing* becomes a gratifying and ambitious habit. You will begin accomplishing with significant swiftness. In turn, it will build your self-confidence and send it soaring. Use the same procedure for psychological pursuits, and I guarantee you, success will follow. Before you know it, you will be managing yourself.

Isn't that the primary aim?

CHAPTER SEVENTEEN

Sure, there will be instances when you find yourself in a situation parallel to a small rabbit in the forest whose pathway is blocked by a sizeable hollow log. By now, you know to expect obstacles, and you're well equipped to handle them. Similar to the long-eared animal, you will have to go over, under, around, or through to reach the other side. At certain junctures, it will be necessary to reverse and take a different route or even modify your destination. First and foremost, do not forget to take a brief step back and reevaluate.

I correlate this procedure with a helpful, daily living tip that I discovered years ago. You may wish to try it. When you want to locate a specific item, usually something small, and you have a general idea where it is, instead of continuing your search with all of the lights on, turn them off. In the dimness, slowly shine a flashlight around the area. Your eyes will focus solely on what's illuminated. More times than not, you will identify exactly what you are looking for. In the process, you will commonly notice things that you had not noticed previously. In the same sense, momentarily stepping back and reassessing your circumstances blocks outer stimuli and spotlights aspects and ideas that you might have otherwise totally overlooked.

When you find yourself passing through a dark tunnel, remember this: *Self-awareness is the avenue to the highway of understanding that enables you to merge onto the interstate of change.* If you become lost or confused, there's nothing wrong with stopping to ask for directions. Licensed therapists and reputable life coaches will always have your back. Additionally, consider hiring a **"fear coach."**

What is a "fear coach"? It's a person who is mentally accomplished and able to effectively impart wisdom and motivation to aid others in conquering their fears. Fear coaches must:

1. love themselves,
2. care about others,
3. be capable of disarming confrontation,
4. have outstanding communication skills,
5. be of strong mind and will, and
6. live healthy lifestyles.

Who makes an excellent "fear coach"? A person who has faced and fought through his or her own fears and has willingly forfeited comfort for discipline in order to excel. Oftentimes those with athletic backgrounds are prime candidates. Having a "fear coach" can be wonderful.

Healthy ambition geared toward personal growth has commonly been undervalued. Yet, a sound peaceful mind is the very key to happiness. True joy comes from contentment within. By understanding that imperfection, failure, and suffering are naturally parts of the human condition, and they can be powerful building blocks for an improved, often exciting, future, you will not remain lost in an undesirable state of despair. Difficulties build resilience when met with an optimistic mentality.

If you have yet to experience major setbacks and challenges, on the one hand, count yourself lucky. On the other, know that when you do, they could prove particularly difficult if you're unprepared. Used to coasting along undisturbed, the first real encounter can come as a solid blow to the gut for anyone. The right mindset makes all the difference. That's what enables a fifteen-year-old to roll with the punches when a thirty-year-old does not and vice versa; it's what helps children and adults adapt. I refer to this part of the brain as the **"resilience muscle**." Everyone has it. How effectively it works is based on how well it is conditioned. Like any muscle, it can atrophy and become weak. Does that mean you have to submit yourself to added difficulties to gain experience? Of course not. It means that you plan ahead by training and developing a strong, resilient mind.

Unquestionably, you've taken on challenging tasks that you have mastered. We all have. When I was ten years old, my father brought home a slightly rusted but shiny red, secondhand bicycle. He patched and inflated the tires. I was chomping at the bit to test it out. My older siblings rode first, and then it was my turn. I could barely reach the pedals while seated, so I leaned forward and stood.

Initially, I rode the bike like a waddling duck. I crashed several times. The wheels resembled a toy gyroscope coming to a halt. Aside from scraped knees and elbows, I was fine. I picked myself up and dusted off. Soon, I was grinning with the contentment of a Cheshire cat while bouncing along our dusty, rutted driveway on two wheels.

Did you learn to ride a bicycle? If so, I'm sure the first few tries were not easy. You were probably a bit panicky, as I was, at the prospect of taking a tumble. However, your perseverance paid off.

Have you ever signed up for a curriculum or taken a class or job that pushed you to your limits, but you nevertheless plowed through? When you had no desire to exercise, did you convince yourself to do it anyway? Have you pushed away from the dining table even though your taste buds craved the enticingly delightful-looking dessert? Do you recall forcing yourself to stay up late? Perchance you wanted to watch the end of an engaging movie or finish an exciting book. Maybe you had to study for a test or prepare a presentation. Perhaps with the gumption of a three-year-old, you fought the urge to sleep for no apparent reason at all. Do you rise and shine at the sound of your alarm clock although you'd rather roll over and continue dreaming?

If you have done any of these, then you know the strength of your own mind. It is a powerhouse. You are your own commander in chief. It's easy to see. The proof is in the pudding. Combine this clear revelation of your built-in might, endurance, and ability to self-direct with the other techniques of my "mental health diet for strength and immunity." You will become less reactive, no longer guided by your impulsive feelings, and more proactive, allowing your intentional, inner presidential initiative to advance.

For all of its protective and wonderful qualities, fear has a sneaky and destructive side. Give it an inch, and it will certainly take a mile. Therein lies the danger. Similar to a ravenous stray animal finally being fed, it's coming back to the same location for more. No matter how tempting it may be, do not feed fear. Reminiscent of signs at the zoo that state, "DO NOT FEED ANIMALS," take a clean sheet of paper and write: "DO NOT FEED FEAR." Post it on your vision board, "brain board," wall, or refrigerator. Taping another copy to the inside of your front door can serve as a powerful reminder before you enter an uncertain world.

Everyone naturally experiences various degrees of fear and anxiety. Years ago, I was guilty of feeding my fear. The more I eased open the door, the more it crept in and took advantage. It occupied too much of my time, and it was leading me as if I were a puppy on a leash. I finally had enough. I eventually decided to name and categorize my experiences.

Fear 1 (external): is visible and mostly created by others. My early childhood ordeal of being locked in the janitor's closet is a prime example.

Fear 2 (internal): is created within and remains there unless one decides to reveal it. The persistent, underlying fear of failure during my first modeling show is a good illustration. In reflection, I held the overwhelming majority of my fears inside.

"Spiking anxiety," however, is different from fear in the fact that it does not linger. It comes on suddenly and generally leaves swiftly, as it did when I first learned to ride a bicycle, and, later on, during my first bodybuilding show.

Are your fears chiefly internal or external? When was the last time "spiking anxiety" caught you by surprise? Does it do so more often than you care to admit? Fears and anxieties naturally transpire, but they don't have to become runaway trains. The advice within these pages is based on my lifetime of observations, experiences, and perseverance.

It's never too late to be ambitious. However, mixing hate with ambition is a recipe for failure. If the downfall doesn't occur right away, it eventually will. Unless you aim to fail yourself and those who care most about you, steer clear of this approach. Instead, become ambitious about improving yourself.

Respect the power of your mind. You are not your thoughts, but they are extremely influential. When you inflame your problems by dwelling on your worries without lifting a finger toward healthy change, you're at a particularly high risk of becoming a victim of your own circumstances. Don't give your brain the ammunition to kill you. If you don't learn to rule negativity, it will beat the hell out of you.

Does that mean you can never complain or talk about your concerns? No. There is nothing wrong with thinking and voicing some negativity as long as you are willing to move forward, and you have a balance of positivity. Life is not always a bed of roses. However, by appreciating the beautiful, vibrant, and pastel hues of the delicate buds and blooms, you balance out the sharp, piercing thorns on the stems.

Hit the ground running—the sooner the better. To kickstart the process, take gratitude in the fact that you are able to think and make decisions. Cling to this gratefulness. Remaining upbeat is therapeutic. What a fantastic way to administer doses of self- encouragement! You now have the tools to do more than merely survive. Use them to thrive.

I believe in you. *You have* endured, *you can* excel, and *you will!* Let your light shine brighter than what you are going through. Remember this: You are the founder, CEO, and president of yourself. Fear no doubt. Rewire and fly higher!

For more insight into the author Likewise, visit:
www.Likewiseoriginal.com

TESTIMONIAL ABOUT LIKEWISE
aka ALEX THOMAS

I'm a biochemist. I consider myself a modern geek with a title. I thought I was a pretty smart guy until I met Alex, whom I have known for about eight years. We met at a basketball game when Alex walked up and asked me if he could give "little man"—referring to my eight-year-old son—a signed basketball poster that had been given to him. It was a heartwarming moment, and my son was overjoyed.

Alex gave my son advice about school and life and had him laughing. My son really took a liking to him. Alex and I talked for about thirty minutes, and we have kept in touch. Infectious, positive energy describes him. From my point of view, his pragmatic, constructive words, and bright, confident demeanor serve to activate the neuro-signaling molecules responsible for general well-being in those around him because everyone he encounters seems to leave in a much better mood. I know I do.

Because of my background, I knew a lot about the human mind, but Alex broadened my view. He explained how wonderful and deadly the mind can become. He says when you are willing to step outside your box, creativity can flow. He taught me it's fine to be proud of what I do, but success is not defined by my job. How many people I touch along the way with what I do is what's important.

When Alex's first book came out—*Ambitious: One Man's Journey to Conquer the Darkness of Dyslexia*—I read it immediately. I had no idea he had endured such hardships. To meet him, you would never know. He would have every right to complain, but he doesn't. It is my honor to have met Alex Thomas, Likewise. I think of him as a friend. I have nothing but respect for him as a man.

Sincerely,
Crow Johnson, PhD

ACKNOWLEDGEMENTS

Thank you, **Indigo River Publishing**, for your dedication and hard work. This book couldn't have reached its full potential without your team of experts. I am forever grateful. Much appreciation goes out to **Executive Editor Deborah Froese** for her understanding and first-class editing skills.

– Likewise, aka Alex Thomas

I want to give special thanks to **Velvet Skies, also known as LuAnn Wibel,** for her help, insight, and sacrifice in creating *Ambitious II*. She earned her bachelor's degree from the University of South Carolina. She has a love for teaching and has spent the last thirteen years working as an educator in Pensacola, Florida.

– Likewise, aka Alex Thomas

CONTACT INFORMATION FOR
SPECIALIZED ASSISTANCE

American Academy of Child & Adolescent Psychiatry
3615 Wisconsin Avenue, N.W.
Washington, D.C. 20016-3007
Email: aacap.org
Tel: 202-966-7300

Anxiety & Depression Association of America (ADAA)
8701 Georgia Avenue
Suite #412
Silver Spring, MD 20910
Email: information@adaa.org

Mental Health America (MHA)
500 Montgomery Street
Suite 820
Alexandria, VA 22314

Tel: 703-684-7722
Toll Free 800-969-6642
Text: "MHA" to 741741

National Alliance on Mental Illness (NAMI)
4301 Wilson Boulevard
Suite 300
Arlington, VA 22203
Tel: 703-524-7600
NAMI Helpline:
Mon. – Fri. from 10 a.m. – 10 p.m. ET
Tel: 1-800-950-NAMI (6264)
Text: "HelpLine" to 62640
Email: -helpline@nami.org
Chat: nami.org/help

Substance Abuse and Mental Health Services Administration (SAMHSA)
5600 Fishers Lane
Rockville, MD 20857
Tel: 1-877-SAMHSA-7 (1-877-726-4727)
SAMHSA (24/7 Assistance):
National Helpline: 1-800-662 HELP (4357)
Suicide & Crisis Lifeline: (call or text) 988
Disaster Distress Helpline: 1-800-985-5990

There are a wide variety of helpful resources available for individuals seeking assistance in the United States and in other countries. Esteemed national organizations provide information and links to local therapists and support groups. Hotlines offer direct aid during a crisis.

www.ingramcontent.com/pod-product-compliance
Lightning Source LLC
Chambersburg PA
CBHW041921090426
42741CB00019B/3441